ISIS WISDOM

Unveiling the Magic of You

Susi Jones

Susi Jones Publishing

Print   ISBN-978-0-9930824-1-2
Digital ISBN-978-0-9930824-2-9

Cover design by: Susi Jones
Illustrations by: Wren B. Jones
Photographer: Benjamin F. Jones

Printed on demand

Dedicated by Goddess Isis

To All on the journey of transformation

CONTENTS

FOREWORD

Unveiling the Magic of You will lead you on a journey of personal and spiritual discovery, it will guide you into refreshing and new ways of thinking and being. The journey will be life changing and life enhancing as you shed those worries and niggling thoughts about yourself and the world around you.

You can choose to read through the book, just gliding through the pages and not actively engaging in the steps advised and I want you to know that this is alright. Your life will be impacted just by reading, as the seeds are sown and your body, mind and spirit begin to remember your magnificence. In the process of writing with Isis, I am transformed and only as I began the process of editing did I actually undertake each of the steps. You have free will, this book came to you at this time, because there is a message here for you, there is a freedom waiting and Isis says " It is my heart's greatest desire to support you through the process of transformation, to discover your magnificence and power"

If you choose to take this journey one step at a time, to follow each step sequentially, then you will gain the greatest insight into your own life. As you uncover the past and find the roots of your story, you can gently guide yourself into all healing. If you choose to deep dive into this journey, give yourself time to assimilate all of the steps and any changes you notice in yourself. There is no rush to your transformation and the speed you take will be right for you.

The book is divided into six Stages of healing on the Journey of Transformation, awakening to your own magnificence which we call Magic. There is a glossary to support your understanding of the terms we use in the book.

Isis was considered magical in her days when known as Goddess Ouset* in Egypt and she wishes you to discover how incredibly powerful you are. We bring this book to you at this time as Earth needs more awakened people to restore balance and heal our civilization.

*This is a phonetic spelling

INTRODUCTION

At this time the world is in flux and there are many old souls that are coming forward to guide and support you all. I lived many years ago in Egypt - I haven't read your stories about me as they are not likely to be the truth as I understand it. If I was to describe my purpose then and now, it was and is to heal. I served the ordinary people, as a healer. I used the Ankh as a tuning fork, to offer the body the vibration of health to show the cells the pathway to health. I was also a medicine woman, I used local herbs, roots, fruits, leaves, flowers and spices to create poultices, balms and tinctures to promote healing and health. The ordinary people were not educated as you are now, they believed stories that were not true and these often led them to self-neglect, sickness and ultimately death. My knowledge came from within me and I was influenced by other healers and medicine of the day.

I am here for a purpose and that is to bring you wisdom to guide your understanding of yourself, the world and where you fit into it. When your eyes are opened you will be unable to unsee, you will seek further knowledge and I encourage you to do this. For reasons I do not understand, your people are not educated in the important wisdom, how earth is, the connection to all that is, to how your energy influences everything and your concern is facing the wrong way. I accept that this might all be news to some and old news to others, yet it is my heart's mission to share wisdom with you and for those who already have opened eyes then take everything you learn here and share it.

I have chosen many people to be my voice, I have chosen people with different skills, connections, interests and belief systems. To hear my words, to translate them into their language and correct mistakes I make through lack of understanding. Susi and I laugh together at my lack of understanding - and I will tell you I love you and find you all fascinating. At times I wonder how you don't know what you don't know and then I look at all the amazing knowledge and skills you have accrued over the years and I am astounded.

When you read the words here, I ask only that you read with an open mind. Not all words will resonate with you, and there will be those that you vehemently disagree with, watch those particular reactions because that is a sign that you have some work to do on that subject.

GLOSSARY

Here you will find some terms that occur in the book and the interpretation of them from Goddess Isis. You will also see the symbol ℗ in the book which indicates the specific companion recording which is available on MP3 for you to enjoy the author guiding you through the meditations. You can also purchase a Companion Journal to record your progress.

All that Is
This is a term used throughout the book in place of Allah, God, Heaven, The Universe, Universal Energy, Yahweh etc.

Breath
There are many references to breathing, this is how you work with your breath to reach different states of being.

Curiosity
This is a key aspect of transformation: it means the desire to know more and the willingness to explore different concepts or ideas.

Fear
Fear is simply the absence of love. There is also a physical response to fear that has great value in a real crisis, however the brain doesn't always turn off this

response and can create limitations and both physical and mental ill health.

Forgiveness
This is a key aspect of transformation: it means to let go of the experience rather than keep living it. Once you have forgiven yourself for holding on so tightly, you may get to a place where you are able to forgive the protagonist. There is no rush or pressure to do this in this lifetime.

Gratitude
This is a key aspect of transformation: Gratitude raises your vibration and transforms your thinking, understanding and responses to life. Simply saying thank you to yourself and others is all it takes.

Healing
Goddess Isis was a healer, she used many different modalities and shares some of these in this book. Many highly evolved and spiritual people experience physical and mental ill health and healing does not necessarily equate to perfect health.

Highest Potential
This is where you are functioning at your optimum level, the best you can be. This is not a static state and will change throughout your journey of transformation.

Highest Wisdom
This is your connection to your spirit, where ego plays no part and the guidance here is pure.

Imagination
This is a key aspect of transformation: it means to create images and experiences in your mind,

beyond your current understanding in order to create something new.

Journal

Using your companion journal or notebook, get into the habit of recording your journey of transformation. Writing can aid the healing process. As words have power which you will see in the Hall of Records keep your journal a place of positive transformation and use scrap paper for letting go of unhelpful thoughts. When you have written all you need, you can burn the scrap paper and write all you have learned in your journal.

Lens

This is a key aspect of personal development: Understanding how we look at life impacts the way we live. There are references to the lens of love, curiosity, imagination etc and we have a choice in every situation to determine the lens we will use.

Love

This is a key aspect of transformation: Love is an element and in every cell of your being. The accepted understanding of love is a veil that once removed will release you from ever feeling unloved.

Magic

This is a word used in the title and throughout the book. This refers to the unknown and magical rather than magic spells and incantations in this context.

Meditation

There are many guided meditations in the book, there is no right or wrong way to meditate, however taking time to be in silence is very healing. You can meditate walking in nature, swimming, sitting or laying but not when driving or using machinery.

Mystery
This is a term that Isis uses for that deep place of silence when the world seems to stand still. It is reached in silent meditation and trance states. You will know this place daily, just before you fall asleep.

Nutrition
There are references in the book to healthy eating and drinking fresh water. Follow medical advice and make informed choices about how you interpret any guidance in the book.

Radiant Golden Light
This is an imagined healing energy from the core of planet earth.

Sacred Space
A dedicated space where you can get lost in wonder and give your body, mind and spirit the space to heal and grow.

Silence
Removing yourself from the noise and chaos of both the inner and outer world in order to restore yourself.

The Golden Thread
This is an imagined healing connection between your physical being and your spiritual connection to All that Is.

Transformation
The intention of this book is that your life is transformed, that you take all of the beauty, knowledge and power that you already are and reveal it to the world, without the programming that has hidden your light.

ISIS WISDOM

Unveiling the Magic of You

UNWRAPPING THE MYSTERY AND MAGIC OF YOU

From wherever you stand right now the journey begins. There are many layers to your existence, many stories that define you and it is important that you know that you are perfect just as you are. You find yourself here because you know there is more to life than this experience of now. It is in the experience of 'knowing' where you will discover how incredibly magnificent you are. And here in this first stage of your journey you will learn how to enter into Mystery, a beautiful place that is always accessible to you. Let us begin.

INTRODUCTION

There is always something really exciting about starting a journey. Packing bags, organising route, transport and making arrangements for the destination. As you begin this journey of Unveiling the Magic of You, you may or may not fully know what that future might look like, but something inside inspired you to explore new possibilities.

Keeping a journal alongside reading this book will enable you to mark your progress, record your questions and experiences and you will see how far you have travelled.

Our first short meditation will centre around the 'destination' the place where you want to be, but first we will explore the basics of meditation that leads us to Mystery.

The Basics Of Meditation

For those for whom this is a new process, please know that there is no right or wrong way to meditate, you can meditate walking in nature or the town, you can meditate in the shower or sitting on a train. Providing you are safe - not driving, caring for young children, cooking or using machinery you will gain something from it.

However, there is wisdom in creating a sacred practice, where you are alone and undisturbed, at a time and place that suits your lifestyle and responsibilities. Create flexibility in your practice because life is full of twists and turns.

As I reflect: Meditation wasn't in my practice, although I did take time out to think and plan and often found myself daydreaming, getting lost in wonder. You might have a practice with a different name and whatever works for you is right for you.

Creating A Sacred Space   Ⓟ1:1

First prepare a time when you will be undisturbed, a place where you will feel safe and comfortable. Bring a glass of water into your space and a journal, you might choose to bring candles, crystals or religious icons or symbols. You might wish to wrap yourself in a blanket, or sit with your back straight in a yoga position. You might wish to bring gentle music or essential oils into this space. You are creating a sacred space and providing yourself with time that other people in your life understand is sacrosanct.

There is wisdom in explaining to others that you need time to yourself, setting a boundary with your family that is understood and will in time be fully respected. This also sends a message that you have started a journey of self discovery. This might raise questions which you must answer in the best way you can without creating risks of your journey of transformation being closed down by others who seek to control you.

Once settled and comfortable:

Relax into the space, straighten your spine, uncross your legs or arms, raise your chin, smile and look for something that catches your attention slightly above your eye line. Let your breath be the conductor at this time, watching how it rises and falls in your chest, noticing the temperature of the breath as it enters and leaves your body. Allowing the tiny muscles around your eyes to relax and when you are ready close your eyes.

Notice as you are watching your breath, how wonderfully warm and relaxed you are beginning to feel. Notice the clothes on your skin, how they gently move with your breath. Become completely aware of the space around your body and notice how your body is feeling.

Do not worry about any thoughts that come to you, when you practice focussing on your breath they will subside. If they are persistent, tell them you will deal with them later, or stop this practice and go and deal with the issue.

Gently begin breathing to a pattern: bringing the breath in through the nose and imagine it filling up your lower belly (this enables your diaphragm to move without your shoulders lifting) and as you breathe out pull your lower belly back in, practise this for a few breaths.

Now breathe in through your nose to a count of 4 and gently breathe out to a count of 7. Practice this for a while until you get into a smooth rhythm and notice how your body relaxes even more. You can breathe out through your nose or your mouth - whichever feels most comfortable.

Meditation: Future You   Ⓟ1:2

As you find yourself drifting into a deep relaxation, enjoying these moments of wonder and calm, we are going on a journey of the imagination. Together we will explore a possible future, where you have reached your destination and have become the person you desire to be.

As you relax here, I want you to look towards a time in the future: Imagine that out there in the distance, you can see a person who looks like you. They are standing on a raised platform and are surrounded by people.

Your curiosity peaks and you rise out of your body and drift over to see yourself in the future. You notice everything - how you are standing, the clothes you are wearing, your shoes, your hair and the people. You watch with awe at the person you have become, exactly as you imagined yourself to be.

You step onto the platform and drift into your future body and it feels comfortable and familiar. You sense the power in yourself that you had dreamed of, you hear the confidence of your voice and notice how it feels to see all these familiar faces and the relationships here, so transformed.

You look back to where you are meditating in wonder and seek the path that led you here, the steps you took. You glide back towards yourself along that path to see each step you took and when you return, drift back into your body. Watching once more the future self you envisioned and remembering all that you need to remember to help you get there. Slowly bring your awareness back to your breath, notice your body, the space around you. As you return, take time to learn all you needed from this time and then write it down in your journal.

Having a dream or a goal will help you to know why and where you are aiming, this is a possible destination, choices based upon your current understanding of now. Maintaining this vision of your future self, will support you on the days when you slip back into old patterns of behaviour or thought. Create something to remind you of this moment that you can keep near you, touch, see or feel to keep the dream alive.

The Journey

When we consider the nature of life, of human life, our understanding comes from great philosophers, scientists and artists. I too was influenced in my understanding and lived through that lens of knowledge which limited my capacity accordingly. But then I learnt how to access the source of all knowledge and that is when I began to use this wisdom to heal people and change my world. I want to share with you a viewpoint that in some ways will be contrary to what you have been told. Take from this what you wish but remain curious and open to possibility:

Life is not quite as you imagine it, how the earth goes round the sun and the clouds form are understood only to a degree. This simple knowledge is interesting and sometimes exciting, yet it is a small drop in the ocean of the truth. The connections between the years, between all the inhabitants of earth and between the world of souls is so rich, complex and yet simple that it would take several lifetimes to partially comprehend.

You might wonder why you chose this book or why the book was gifted to you - is there a greater force behind the why, what or who was this choice inspired by? The answer might remain a mystery and if so can you live with that?

You are human, being human brings with it many great gifts, you are made of flesh and blood and you are an amazing machine with incredible capacity. Some people stretch their bodies to full capacity and others stretch their minds. Is this all you are? Do you remember when you were growing, first noticing your body, your difference as you compare yourself to others, do you remember wondering why your eyes were that colour and your hair was that way? And as you grew, you wondered how you would fit into the world and how it would mould around you?

Do you remember wondering where you went when daydreaming? Those thoughts and voices that played in your head, the imagination of play and your toys speaking to you? When you are very young, life is magical, a mystery, full of the unknown, full of hope and aspiration. Conversations with your toys and the creatures you met along the way, the world was a stage on which you learnt to navigate your body and mind into thrills and excitement. And then....you were told what to think, what was right or wrong, silly or serious. And the decline in your capacity began.

Can you find the magic and mystery of your childhood amidst all that 'knowledge' you have gained. Depending on where you are on your spiritual quest will determine how much unveiling you require.

The simple way to discover the magic of you is to create an Intention, to give it time and focus and maintain practices that will lead you towards your desired goal. How you choose to do this is very personal and even if you just want to read on and not think too hard about anything, you will transform just by the reading of these words.

The biggest veil on earth is that you are a separate being, that you alone need to find your way. The truth is that you are far from alone, you are guided, encouraged and supported every step of the way. There is a connection between you and your Highest Wisdom, and here in this chapter it is our intention that you understand that connection and know how to use it. With this connection you open up the opportunity of living at your highest potential.

A Well Of Love

Deep inside you there is a well, a well of love that you and others can draw from. This well of love is so pure, so clean, so free from everything that is happening in the body. It is the source - the very essence of all that you are.

This well of love was inside you before you were born, like a rivulet that flows from the deepest parts of you into each cell of your body, it infuses you with power, confidence, assurance and knowledge of your connection to All that is . (God, Allah, The Universe, Universal Energy etc)

When you access this well of pure wholesome love, you are at your most powerful. The concerns, worries and fears evaporate into it and are purified.

You connect to this source of love deep inside you through your breath, as you journey through this book you will revisit the breath and learn more, but for now, consider how you breathe, focus in on your breath without need to change. As you go about your day fulfilling all those tasks watch your breath, how it changes, how much of your lungs you are using.

When you breathe in we call it inspire, you breathe in the air and your spirit, this is your access point to this source of love deep inside you.

When you breathe out we call it exhale, which is expired air. You can use this natural process to let go of anything that ceases to be valid in your life, like old stories, fears, frustrations, disease.

When we use the breath in a conscious way - we can amplify it with an intention - this is when we are aiming towards a chosen goal, a dream or an aspiration etc.

A Simple Exercise   Ⓟ1:3

When you have a few moments to focus only on your breath: Sit upright, supported, both feet on the floor and hands unlocked on your lap. Lift your chin a little and smile.

Consider a state you wish to achieve like, peace, calm, enthusiasm, motivation etc. Bring your attention to the breath and rest with it, watching it. Now breathe in through your nostrils and out through your nostrils relaxing your jaw and tongue. Imagine the breath coming into the source of love deep inside you in your mind, speak out your intention, add detail and the desired outcome. Imagine this source of love receiving the intention.

Continue breathing in this mindful way and then bring your attention back to your body and open your eyes. Drink water to enhance the experience, write in your journal and go about your day noticing how your intention begins to evolve in surprising ways.

Create a routine that allows you to practice this simple meditation regularly. The more familiar you are with your breath and the connection to the source of love deep within you, the greater your understanding will be as you journey through the book. You are now connecting to your Highest Wisdom, and as you go further on in your journey you will discover more and build stronger bonds.

Boulders, Barriers & Limitations

Do you believe 'There are events, people and limitations that prevent you from going in the direction of your dreams'? Can you reframe that to: 'There are events, people and limitations that guide my path, enable me to heal my broken parts and to grow in strength as I move forward in the direction of my dreams'? Life is all about perception, the lens through which you experience the world around you.

On the journey of awakening, you will meet up with many Boulders, Barriers and Limitations. These might be

Angels dressed in ragged clothes, the beggar on the street that you help, leaving you late for your appointment. The woman struggling in the queue without sufficient money for their goods. The minor accident that delays your plans, relationships that blow up or fizzle away. Close family and friends sickness or death. There are hundreds if not thousands of events that seemingly are boulders or barriers that prevent you moving forward.

A Boulder is something that blocks your way, prevents you from moving in that direction. On the journey of awakening or transformation, you can choose to look at this through a different lens, in fact play with the lenses that you create to see what you learn. We will explore lens and filters in depth in the next stage, for now play with the idea and imagine you have a different pair of glasses for each mood.

Choose a 'boulder' that is blocking your way: Put on the Lens of 'it's not fair': What do you learn from that? Now try the Lens 'nothing ever goes my way': What do you learn from that? Try on the Lens of Love: now how do you see it? Try on the Lens of 'maybe this Boulder is a friend and will stop me going in the wrong direction': is this possible? Changing perception is not about someone telling you, it's about making your own choice, finding your path until it all makes sense and is comfortable.

A Barrier prevents you from doing something you wanted to, here are some examples: Unrequited Love: when the person you love does not reciprocate, that is a barrier to your dreams. A barrier can be protective or it can be there for you to rise up against it, or to find a way to remove that barrier, to negotiate your way through or around it. You might want the latest 'model....' and your barrier is lack of financial resources to buy it. How do you choose to perceive this? 'It's not fair' or " Ok if I save 'x' amount of money each month I will be able to afford it by 'Month' or some other thought that moves you towards your goal.

Limitations might include, failing a job interview, being dismissed, not getting into the university or college course. Not finding love or finding that you do not have the skills to follow an aspect of your dream. Often the

11

limitations are in your mind and under your control: I cannot, I should not, I must not, I will never, I'm not worthy, I'm stupid, I'm useless, I will never be any good at...., I will never find love. You know your story: are you ready to change it?

Simple Steps

Listen with open ears to 'self speak'. Explore if this belief was true in the past. Ask yourself whether this is true today. Explore how this might limit you going forwards. Ask loved ones if they believe that this is true. Bring the belief to meditation: Set your intention to eradicate the belief and find a replacement that empowers, protects and leads you forwards. Using your breath to relax your body and mind. When you are ready, speak your intention in your head or out loud.

Listen to see if you receive any guidance, don't worry if you can't 'hear' anything, you might have a sense of something, or a feeling. Sometimes your thoughts and ideas click into place and you can see the bigger picture.

When you are ready, bring yourself back into the present. Write in your journal all that you have learned. Create a new statement to replace the old, some people call these Affirmations or Mantras. Write down the new statement and place it in a prominent place to remind yourself and when you slip into the old story, notice. When you notice - say the new story as loud as you can in your head or into the air.

You can repeat this process each time you notice any limiting beliefs. Take your time, there is no rush.

Protagonists In Your Story

You will hold many people responsible for your limiting beliefs. The words they spoke will echo in your mind until you do the work. The story you tell yourself will have grown, you might have embellished it with the telling, exaggerated it, or hidden aspects of it.

The protagonist, the person who said those words, often a parent, teacher or leader or an influential person in some way is completely oblivious to your plight. Is it possible that the words you heard were relevant within the context of that moment? Is it possible they didn't actually think that about you but about your behaviour at that time?

Have you considered their own personal circumstances, fears, worries, concerns that might have influenced their reaction and response to you at that time?

Follow The Steps Above And Add These:

Bring the protagonist to mind, see their face and look into it. What was happening in their life at the time? Hold an imaginary conversation with them and ask them what they meant and if it was true or just their frustration at the time that caused them to speak those words.

Listen without judgement, don't worry if there is silence, rest in it and allow your highest wisdom to intervene. With this deeper understanding: Forgive yourself for holding on so long to that idea. Forgive the protagonist for their part related to this event.

Imagine that you can wrap those words in Love, that all the pain they caused and the damage to your relationship with the protagonist can be transmuted into a new story and new possibilities.

THE POWER OF CONNECTION

In order to unwrap the bonds and binds that hinder you, it will be necessary to consider the people in your life. I invite you to add an interesting consideration to human relationships:

Scientists will tell you that Earth vibrates at 7.83Hz and Humans in a healthy state vibrate at 7.83Hz, this tells us that when we are functioning we are in harmony with Earth. When we experience dysfunction, our vibration changes. In the music you listen to, you are aware of the different 'vibes' associated with each piece, you know this because you echo that vibration and your emotions, feelings and mood change accordingly.

You choose your music according to the desired state you wish to achieve. You might want to dance, or sing along or maybe relax with your eyes closed. If we think of people and relationships in this way we can powerfully change our relationships by playing their music, we can stop taking things personally and we can start seeing the other person's greater needs.

A Simple Exercise

Make a list of people closest to you, then create a list of emotions that you feel regularly. Go through the list of people and assign an emotion you 'generally' feel when you are with them. Ask yourself how each relationship is supporting your growth, your vision and your goals.

It is easy to assume that someone who irritates you is not 'good for you'. Consider that they may be exactly what you need to keep you motivated. In your meditation practice, bring each person to mind, start with gratitude, all the things you are grateful for then bring to mind your memories, experiences and emotions and extract all the learning from your relationship without judgement.

The Same Simple Exercise In Reverse

Make a list of the important people in your life and think about the emotions you generate in them. What gifts are you bringing to each relationship? Are you supporting their growth? Are you a boulder, barrier or limitation or champion of their dreams?

Bring each person into your meditation practice and imagine you can make a connection with their energy to discover how best you can serve them, what music they need right now? Create a new relationship with them based on all you have learned. Keep them close to your heart every day and send love and gratitude in your daily practice.

It is through the dynamic of these relationships that you are formed and the shape of your life tomorrow will be created by your movement forward from this moment.

Human relationships are the reason you are here today, the reason you are on or off purpose, and all of the people in your life are there for a reason. You will learn later on about the sacred contracts you made with others to support each other's growth, but for now, let us just imagine this to be the truth. Do not make value judgements, as each person has a purpose be it significant or insignificant to your life. Many of these people will have contracted to play a part - lead you down a path. Some people have agreed to play a role that has brought great learning, often painful yet life transforming, some stay for a long time and many just a short time.

The seeds sown through all of these connections will flourish where they need to, where the ground is right. Just by 'being' not necessarily by any doing, you will bring light, dark, health, dis-ease, comfort or pain to many people, as you too were contracted to sow these seeds or maybe till the soil for the people you meet.

Many Seek 'The One'

Humans need companionship, intimacy and the security of being in partnership with another. This may or may not be a sexual relationship. Intimate relationships are often formed with members of your soul family, be it for comfort or learning. Sexual relationships without intimacy are generally walk-ins, like bit parts in a film. When you seek The One - that soulmate/twin flame, that deep connection with another, there are steps to take.

A Simple Exercise To Explore Your Hearts Desire

Write a list of all that you desire in a life partner (Not a list of attributes like: handsome/pretty). Think about what you need: If you're grounded and safe but need something more adventurous, then you might seek an adventurer that loves a solid home base.

Write a separate list of all the gifts you bring to the relationship. Now compare the lists and write down what you learn. IF you want an adventurer, then start now to create adventures. You are more likely to meet The One if you have shared interests -whatever they are.

If you need someone to pamper you,pamper yourself. If you need to hear the words I love you - tell other people that you love them - they will eventually reciprocate. Every day in your writing, add some details about your need for a deep and meaningful relationship.

And every day massage your feet and tell them how grateful you are for them and send them love. And in your heart and mind be grateful for The One wherever they are or whatever they're doing and send them love.

Life Partners

In a culture where you have freedom to choose your life partner, make sure you choose well. Lean on those who truly love you and want the best for you and seek their guidance.

When you meet another, look beyond the image that the new relationship projects and seek the heart of their thoughts, beliefs and actions. Consider their music, their vibrational energy as it rises and falls to different stimuli, go beyond the physical attraction to explore the heart of them.

Using your intuition, instincts and heart, move forwards gently. Be in silence with them and sense their ease, get to know their levels of maturity within different scenarios and contexts. If you want children, observe them in the company of children. Open up the conversation of child rearing, responsibility and the inevitable changes in relationship dynamics

How does this new relationship respond to your hobbies, your 'life interests', your family and friends, working hours and habits? Can you trust this person to hold up the mirror of truth for you, and can you sit with their pain and hold them in love throughout and will they honour you with the same love? Relationships take time to grow, as you learn more about each other allow space for transformation and learning.

Whether arranged or free, you make a choice every day to make the relationship work. Choose to find all that is lovely about them, focus on their strengths and avoid the pit of criticism and irritation.

A Healthy Intimate Relationship

A healthy relationship requires an intention: to Love. Take time to build an understanding of each other, to learn how to be together in partnership, to make unilateral decisions and to seek the best path for you both - individual and collective

A relationship is not like 2 rivers that meet and become one wider river, it is like 2 rivers that run parallel with rivulets connecting them for intimate exchange. Two individuals on their path, going roughly in the same direction whilst maintaining their unique sovereignty.

A relationship that offers a mirror up to each other to support transformation and spiritual and personal development. A shared path of love and for those who choose to create children, work out your beliefs and expectations in order that you can give your children a balanced and healthy start in life.

Choose to love with each exchange, with each flaw or irritation, choose only to love. Seeing your partner whole, healthy, vibrant and functioning and maintaining that through any difficulties will speed the process of their healing. Focusing on negativity will separate you from them.

There will be times when one partner needs more support than the other and willingly you will serve each other at that time. If the balance tips due to long term sickness, then remember you are partners in love and if you are able to get support for the caring in order that you can maintain the love relationship then do so.

We have explored love in relationships with other humans, let us return to the beginning when we talked about your relationship with your highest wisdom and the well of love that you can access and further develop that bond.

The Golden Thread

I am introducing you to a concept that may or may not be new to you: You are a physical being, you have a mind, with the capacity to think, learn and forget. You are connected to a higher wisdom, you might call this: Spirit, Soul, God, The Universe, Universal Energy, All that Is or maybe something else.

Assuming this concept is correct, I want to talk to you about

How to connect to this higher wisdom.

Simple Steps To Connect To Your Highest Wisdom

If we create an imagined space outside of earth's atmosphere in the cosmos, you can call it heaven or something else, I will use All that Is for simplicity. Imagine that a part of you lives there:

We will call this your highest wisdom. In All that Is, the highest wisdom of every sentient being are grouped together. There are many groups and they gather information, create, learn and teach. These groups have different experiences and make different choices for individuals and the collective need. They are highly collaborative and operate solely on love. Because of this there is no polarity and therefore no conflict. Everything that occurs is examined and valued equally as an opportunity to gather more information and further develop creative understanding.

Your 'Soul Energy' returns to this place after it has concluded all its learning on Earth. Whilst your soul energy is in human form, it is connected to All that Is through an imagined golden thread. This links from the heart centre to the Highest Wisdom, which links to All that Is. Information is carried backwards and forwards along this golden thread.

When you activate this golden thread in periods of silence, meditation and breathwork, you bring into your own body a stream of love. This is pure essence love which means that it is different from human love, it has no 'need' attached, it flows freely and supports your highest potential. It also has the capacity to get you back on track, if that is your intention. It can also support healing of the body, mind and restore what you refer to as spirit. The concept of All that Is, the imagined space and the golden thread are fundamental to this journey and even if on reading this you find it challenging, remain open to possibility.

Meditation & Mystery

The more you enter into the practice of meditation, the easier it will be to get into the state of Mystery which is a vibrational state between wakefulness and sleep. A place that is silent, where thoughts cease and you can experience a sense of nothingness, with a sense of deep peace.

It can take many hours of practice to fully enter into Mystery and remember you have a lifetime, so take time, enjoy the process and what you cannot achieve in meditation yet, just imagine you can.

Simple Steps   Ⓟ1:4

In your imagination, see yourself sitting or laying in a deep meditation. Imagine from your heart centre you can see a golden thread stretching out and up into the cosmos. Zoom in on the golden thread to see what is happening: Can you imagine that it is energetic, moving, as if alive? This is love energy streaming down from the cosmos as a golden light into the heart of you.

Now zoom in with X-ray vision at your body and follow the golden light coming into your heart centre and radiating deep within. Imagine you can see a 'flame' in the centre of your body? Is it white gold light? Can you see the golden light merging with the 'white gold flame of light' within?

Notice now your body as it is breathing in and out, slowly, mindfully and relaxed. Imagine that you can notice the golden light leaving your body through your skin, your nose, your higher heart, head and feet and filling the space around you. The space around you filled with golden light gets bigger as more love energy flows into you, through you out into the world.

When you experience this and become familiar with

the process, you can use this energy to fill your home, the community where you are, the landmass and the world.

Now bring yourself back into the present moment and review what you have imagined. You have now imagined the source of connection between your soul energy in your physical being and your Highest Wisdom linked to All that Is through the golden thread and have seen the golden light, love energy and the white gold flame of light within your body.

You can use this visualisation to build connection with your highest wisdom and as you form bonds with this deeper aspect of all you are, you can draw upon the infinite knowledge of who you are, why you chose to be here, your purpose and what steps you need to take on your journey.

Your Highest Wisdom will not tell you lottery numbers, or predict the future and will not interfere with your life choices. The reason for this is because you are collecting data to process and whatever you decide to do, the information will further the evolution of mankind and Earth.

Building these bonds takes time and as you journey through the stages of Unveiling the Magic of You, you will release more stories, beliefs and limitations you have gathered through the years.

There is no rush, you are here now and like all healthy and sustainable relationships, take it slowly, learn gently and allow time to assimilate any changes. Also remember there is no right or wrong way to unveil, to enter into mystery or to discover the magnificence or magic of who you truly are.

Entering Into The Mystery Of The Heart The Golden Thread

Deep inside your heart is the key to how you choose to live your life. It impacts on the amount of complex difficulty you can manage and how your ego plays out in the world.

The key to a healthy heart is through the golden

thread which enters just above your heart and is the place where love enters into you from universal energy and your soul energy. Acupressure practitioners call this spot the sea of tranquillity. To activate this key, requires a daily practice of connecting to All that Is. Just as you plug in your devices to charge them, you need to do the same. Running on empty damages the device, running on empty damages your body, mind and spirit.

Immerse yourself daily in golden light and soak yourself, that it might not only cleanse your cells and heal you, but also fill you with love and allow you to see the world through that lens. When you are looking at the world through the lens of love, your ego and former heartbreaks are held back. Your desires for conflict, difficulty and separation are held back.

This lens has no need for judgement and will always seek ways to bring peace and harmony. This lens will protect you from hurt and rather than taking things personally, it will show you the places inside that need healing. You can then react, not by expressing your pain to another, but by bringing that pain to Source Energy for understanding and healing.

Simple Steps Ⓟ1:5

Take time every day to sit or lay in a safe place where you will be undisturbed. Notice your breath, rising and falling, notice the sounds of the space you are in and any aromas there. Notice the clothes resting on your body and your body relaxing with every breath.

Breathe in, hold, gently release and repeat, keep breathing slowly until you feel calm and at peace allowing any thoughts to roll by like a cloud in the sky. Imagine the golden thread coming from the sky and touching you just above your heart. Notice the golden light coming into your body and infusing every cell and as you breathe out that the golden light is leaving your body and encasing you. Stay here, receiving this beautiful healing light and watching the light surround you.

You may notice wisps of darker energy leaving your body, these will be the hurts that you are holding that do not need attention, the pains in your body that are stuck and no longer have value. When you are completely filled and the golden light around you is bright and still. Bring to mind any concerns you are carrying and ask All that Is to guide and heal your journey. Trust that this will be done and now simply bask in this beautiful light.

IF you need an added protection because you are facing difficulties, you can imagine a pot of molten metal: gold, silver or platinum being poured over your energetic field and encasing the golden light around you. In this protective space, receive the golden light of love and see yourself entering into the perceived difficulty with this power and protection. Notice all that you notice, see others through this lens, see their weakness, their ego, their fears and send them love.

When satisfied that you understand what to do: Bring your attention back to your breath, become aware of the sounds in the space, the aromas, the clothes on your body and bring yourself back into the space. Stay quiet for a while and drink water to cleanse you.

Write the solutions you have discovered in your journal.

Radiant Golden Light

You have learned about the golden thread and the golden light that you can access from All that Is. You can also connect with the energies of earth, you are aware of earths' power, how it sustains life and how it has seen civilisations come and go. Earth remains, it is self-sustaining, able to evolve, as it is a living, breathing expression of life that has the capacity to heal itself.

When you make connections with earth, you can align with its energy and work in harmony to bring peace and hope to all of earth's inhabitants. The vibrational energy of earth is love, as the very fabric of earth is love. You can draw from this energy every time you are in mystery or walking in nature. You can connect with All that Is, here on earth by making connection with the ground, plantlife, trees, oceans, rivers, animals, insects, birds. All on earth resonate with her energies as they share her frequency otherwise they wouldn't be visible here.

All life vibrates, our ability to see colours, each other and objects relates to the speed or frequency of our vibration. As you raise your vibration therefore it will increase what you can see and hear and the higher you rise, the denser and darker energies on earth no longer hold their power over you.

Radiant Golden Light is the love light that emanates from Earth. It is the source of life here and will shine for eternity. When you tap into this source of love and bring in the radiant golden light with the golden light through the golden thread, you become a beacon of love and shine bright for all to see.

Simple Steps   Ⓟ1:6

If you are able: immerse yourself in nature or create an image of nature that you love. Go into mystery, through the breath until you are as deep in as you can go today. Imagine that you can travel into the ground below, through the top layers of soil and rocks and deep into the layers below. Notice what you notice, the creatures that live here, the roots of plants and trees, the mycelium network and going deeper now, the layers of crystal and streams of water.

Enjoy this magical journey creating images from memory or imagination of earth's layers. Notice the deeper you go, you can feel the warmth and light embracing you and you feel a deep sense of peace resting here. Rest here a while and stay for as long as you wish.

In your imagination return back to the place you are sitting, bring through your heart centre the golden light through the golden thread and fill your body and the space around you.

Now imagine that you can pull radiant golden light

from earth up into the base of your spine and let it travel up and into your head, imagine it shooting out into the sky above you and then falling back around you so that you have this beautiful image of light coming from above, below and merging together in and around you. Sit here in this wonder for as long as you can, allowing the silence to enter into you to cleanse any thought concerns you are carrying.

Allow the energy of All that Is in the universe and on earth fill you to overflowing with love. As this radiates in, through and out of you, imagine each cell of your body healing itself. As you practise these simple steps as often as you have the time, you will speed up the process and become aware of the transformation within you. You have now taken the first steps to Shining Bright.

Magical

You are magical, although this might be a word used for spells, incantations and the dark arts, these are only representations of dominance and fear. Every human is magical or supernatural, full of mystery and wonder.

Consider the way you are created and designed, how your body heals itself to maintain harmony within each cell, to filter thoughts and information, to procreate, to love, to nurture and to create. These are the skills of no ordinary creation, you are incredible, magical and superwonderful.

You create in your imagination: consider the amazing architecture, vehicles, machinery, art, writings that are in your experience. All of these started with an idea, a thought and think of the millions of thoughts you have in a day and mostly discard. How did you choose the thoughts to hold, to develop and create from?

When you think of words like supernatural, what are your first thoughts? Do you see spectres, witchcraft, or do you see that which is not fully understood as a superpower? What is your superpower? What are you exceptional at? Or is this buried so deep that you have no concept of it? When you were born, you had this superpower and now it is time to uncover it again.

Simple Steps

Go about your days as normal, there is no need to change anything, become the observer of your life, create an investigative and curious mindset. Notice everything: what you see, what you ignore, what you hear, how you respond. Where you 'feel' things in your body, map this out in your body, write down or record key learnings.

Play with this for a few days, what have you learned about yourself? Bring this to your time of Mystery, create an intention to understand the essence of who you are. Repeat the process regularly.

Each person has their own 'essence' their 'superpower', this is not competitive, or a time to compare. Some people's superpowers will become public knowledge, others will live quietly touching the hearts and minds of the people they meet.

You do not need to be able to 'name' your magical powers, you need to 'live them'. Other people can define you as they will, but for you it is enough to keep practising and perfecting your powers. As you develop your power, you might notice that the world seems brighter, in higher definition, as if you are taking away a filter from your eyes and ears.

You might find that you are connecting to your heart centre and feeling new energy here. This energy pulses power through you and creates a sense of fullness and peace. You are beginning the journey of connecting to universal energy , God energy, All that Is, Source and whichever words align with you, they are all the source of love.

Love is pulsing through you, it is real, energetic, life giving. It rises from the earth, it's in the air, the fruit and vegetables you eat, it comes through your heart from All that Is and from earth herself. Imagine your 'battery pack' is a light within you, you charge this up daily with Love. You maintain your battery pack with sunlight, water, clean air and connection to All that Is. This 'light within you' is magical, it is the source of your superpower, it is soul energy, the infinite aspect of you. You are a soul having a physical experience. This is THE MAGIC OF YOU.

The light within is for yourself and the world. You are here for a purpose and that is to expand knowledge and understanding about the human experience. There will be a time to shine your light and a time to keep it inside. This takes discernment to know when and where to use the light. For now, keep it to your own learning and when people start to notice the changes in you, then it will be time to find your own way to talk about your experience.

You might read books of other people sharing their transformation story, do not compare yourself with others, the people you reach need your story and all these experiences are of great value and influence the evolution of earth.

Curiosity And Imagination

These are two very important skills you need for this journey of transformation on the path to awakening to your superpower.

Simple Steps To Curiosity

Recognise the stumbling blocks that stopped your childlike curiosity, be inquisitive, ask questions, pretend you don't know . Make up fantastical explanations and have fun with "What if... The sun could talk, humans had wings, dreams are other lifetimes. What would happen if.....? Be playful, experience life with all its wonder. Invite others to debate ideas: What do you think about.....? Why are we taught that....? If you could fly - where would you go..?

These 'flights of fancy' will raise your vibrational energy and dispel any denser low mood energy and you will experience more joy, laughter and freedom.

Simple Steps To Building Imagination ⓟ1:7

Imagination is a non-physical creative superpower, play with your imagination and have fun until you laugh out loud.

Choose a real life thing: e.g. A butterfly. Start by building an image in your mind, colour it, decorate it, create dialogue or sounds, create movement, create a story around it.

Choose a hobby you want to perfect e.g running: Sit down and breathe, getting deep into Mystery. See yourself in your running clothes, on the path, notice who you are with: Your favourite sports person, your younger self, your older self. Notice the temperature and the terrain, begin your journey, notice how you are keeping up with your younger self, notice how your favourite sports person is running a step in front of you and in your mind's eye see yourself finishing first. Up your pace, feel the wind behind you, your feet not touching the floor, your muscles and limbs moving effortlessly, your heartbeat calm and regular, your breathing controlled and effortless. You are slightly ahead of your favourite sports person and you're both laughing as you cross the finish line first. Hear the cheers and the laughter and bring yourself back into your space. What did you learn from this exercise of Imagination?

Curiosity and Imagination are key skills to Unveiling the Magic of You. These are innocent qualities that challenge your conditioning. Your superpowers as a young child were curtailed by education and culture, you might consider why these qualities did not fit the accepted narrative of the day. You might spend time searching for meaning and find yourself disappointed and angry. This would be a waste of energy and time, when you enter into being annoyed at what you cannot change... in this case the past, then you are in the opposite energy to Love which is light, effervescent and solution focussed. It is much more constructive to build, to move forward in time to build a future that will sustain you and help the evolution of the planet.

NAVIGATING
THE WORLD

As you have learned already, at birth you understood a great deal and as you grew, this understanding was marred by the culture, education and life experiences you had, this at best left you confused. Many young souls get frustrated because in All that Is, thoughts become things very quickly and on earth that doesn't happen with the speed of light and sometimes not at all.

You are shaped and moulded by your family, your beliefs are created by mimicking your families behaviours and actions and you learn to comply rather than face difficulties. You learn through observation and as a child you live a great deal in the stories created in your mind. These stories are fantasies playing out for you to learn and grow in understanding.

The joy of youth is experimentation, as you choose different clothes, different music, styles of language and behaviours, meet up with people who live a diverse life who have been shaped and moulded by other parents. This highly creative state allows you greater freedom of expression and as you grow into adulthood the world opens up.

Of course when you walk the narrow path of your culture and family there is great safety, everyone understands what you understand. You know what is allowed and what is not, how far you can take risks and how much freedom of expression you are allowed.

When out in the world, fending for yourself, the pressures increase. There is less time to live in your head creating stories, as now you are improvising every moment to learn about the world and where you fit. You are entering into deeper relationships, moulding yourself to fit, to be accepted, to be loved. You might wish to act out the stories of your childhood, or you might reject them and choose a completely different path.

Hitting up against comparison, conflict and difficulty, financial concerns, educational and employment concerns are all realities of adulthood. Should you choose a life partner and become a parent, then you have new responsibilities that will add pressure to life.

At the same time you are likely to maintain links with your family and have to defend your choices. Life is a rich tapestry of learning, if you were to assign a coloured thread for each person, each experience, a beautiful chaotic and creative image would be stitched and would evidence the amazing experience of life on earth.

Navigating The Spiritual Path

When you seek a deeper meaning to life, have a knowing that there is something missing and you seek an understanding of your life from a spiritual perspective, there are many paths to follow.

You will be influenced by people who are on their spiritual path. This may be through formal religious groups who offer attractive communities or you might find your path through an internet search, watching YouTube, reading books, attending workshops or meeting with others.

When you are seeking this deeper meaning to life, your highest wisdom in partnership with All that Is will bring information to your attention, provide opportunities for learning and offer experiences that support your journey. The deeper you delve into the spiritual world, you will find yourself questioning what you are being shown, and this is good. The gift of discernment is valuable at this time. Rather than make any commitments, stand back and observe, do not be caught up in the fervour of the moment, ask questions and bring all your learning through the golden thread in your meditation practice.

The deeper you find yourself in learning with a commitment to study and practice new skills, the changes in you will become apparent. Your lifestyle, behaviours, judgements and energy will have shifted. People will begin to question as you begin to glow from the inside and people feel drawn to you.

You may also face opposition as the people who you used to engage with might no longer be a good fit with your new way of being. Your family and close friends might feel offended that you are rejecting their model of living. Navigating the world as a spiritual being is not always easy and may indeed bring conflict to you.

Simple Steps To Understanding Conflict

Infuse yourself with radiant golden light daily, protect yourself by bringing all of your experiences to your sacred space for healing and guidance. Welcome all challenges as a mirror: When people show their broken places to you, they are often showing you your own broken places. Bring this learning to your sacred space and invite the radiant golden light to heal you.

Express gratitude to all of your mirrors, forgive yourself for any part you played in the exchange, forgive the other for their part in the exchange. Examine your learning and imagine life without that broken place and how to act as you heal.Bring yourself out of meditation, drink water and journal your learning. The spiritual path leads you to follow the path of your purpose that you designed before you were born. There will be many opportunities for learning along the way and you might wonder when you will be free from the learning.

The journey of transformation will continue throughout your infinite life. In this body it will end when you leave it. However, day by day, as you grow and learn you will see the riches and blessings of a spiritual life and welcome the conflict and challenges as the next step in your transformation.

Imagine how many pieces of information you gather every day, far too many to recollect. You collect sufficient information for your learning and disregard the rest. This means that you will be disregarding many lessons and only noticing what is important at this time. Trust that your Highest Wisdom and All that Is will provide opportunities on the next step of your path and that everything happens for a reason and you are free to choose how you react or respond.

Forgiveness

On the journey of transformation you will bump up against many old stories. These stories carry the energy of your past and any emotions that were present in them are triggered by recall and echoes will be present today.

Each time you smell freshly cut grass, or the scent of a rose, you are generating a pathway from the very first time you became aware of it to now and the feelings that you feel today conjure up memories of all those times you experienced this. If you are a visual person you might see yourself in that first image, or 'feel that feeling so strongly' or 'hear the sound of the lawn mower'.

What you might think of as warm and fuzzy feelings, that leave you with a smile on your face and a flutter in your body are powerful and raise your vibration of love.

When the recall is painful, shocking, filled with hurt, guilt, loss or shame then you live on high alert and the vibration of these feelings, the images and sounds on the screen of your mind are in high definition are revisited with the smallest stimuli. This is the vibration of Fear and the antidote is Love.

Any journey from A to B requires a sacrifice, a sacrifice of time, energy and focus. A journey from Fear to Love requires sacrificing the old story, making a commitment to yourself to make a connection with your highest wisdom daily. To practice loving yourself and filling yourself with love from All that Is throughout your day. Noticing what triggers memories and where this is present in your body, vision or mind.

As you embark on this journey of transformation, as you unveil these stories to reveal the mystery of who you really are, they will lose their potency. The triggers will be understood and you will know the 'how to' manage them. One of the keys to transformation is learning the art of forgiveness. Forgiveness is an artform, it is unique to you, you will sculpt and form the pathway, like a river running its course and being redirected by the landscape.

Forgiveness is an intimate and personal practice, it starts by understanding yourself, by choosing to find love for yourself in small and large ways. It continues with self care, with managing your life and relationships with a foundation of love, allowing love to grow within you every day. By giving yourself permission to choose the lens of love and to notice when you swap out with the lens of fear.

As you build the scaffolding of love, then and only then can you begin to unpack the story. You might choose to work with another who has been on this journey, who is skilled in transformation work and forgiveness. You must choose which is the best path for you as you begin to change the screen in your mind from high definition to grainy and grey images until they fade away into the memory archive.

Recognising that each potent story has other players in it, there will come a time in the unravelling where you will need to let go of their part. Holding on to the energy of the past, holds that person in stasis. It is likely that they have no recall of that event, either because they have buried it deep within them or because they have done the work of forgiving themselves. But holding on to the emotions and feelings, the movie holds you back from living a life at your highest potential.

Most children have a story that has had a major impact in their lives, often words spoken in the heat of the moment or heard incorrectly. These words created a lens and a belief which many adults still wear. It is likely that you remember the protagonist and have a negative view of them.

You may have created a sculpture of them and held them in stasis. When you unpack these stories and begin to see them from the standpoint of the speaker, see the situation they were in, the lens that they were wearing at the time, then it is easy to let them off the hook. And more importantly let yourself off the hook.

Notice when you say 'I can't' or 'I'm no good at...' or 'I will never be.....' These probably have a story attached to them. It will not be necessary to speak to the protagonist of any of your stories, the letting go is for your journey, your healing and your freedom. You may ask "Will it have an impact on them?" Yes it will because when people are held in stasis their lives can be impeded without understanding. When you set them free, they have the opportunity to do their own work.

Simple Steps ℗1:8

Take yourself into Mystery as deep as you can go. Ask All that Is to bring in guides, angels or beings to support you, tell them you have a story that you want to unravel and ask for help to set yourself and other players free.

Focus on your breathing, bring to mind the other player and imagine a cord that connects you. Imagine the other person drifting further away into the distance until they are in the mist. Put your hand on your heart centre and imagine you can gently pull out all of the cord that has wrapped around your heart like the roots of a tree. Notice your heart relaxing as it is released, filling with blood, pumping in rhythm and notice any trigger feelings slowing down.

Fill yourself with radiant golden light and let it fill the space around you.Imagine the other person out there in the mist encased in a ball of light, take hold of the cord that you have pulled out and let it go.At the same time in your mind see the other drifting away and the cord breaking down into smoke like vapour and disappearing into the air.

Tell yourself that you are much loved and on your

journey to transformation. Breathe in love from All that Is, from the earth and from all those that love you. And finish this moment of mystery by saying "I love you" to yourself.

Go gently for the rest of the day, drink water, find time in sunshine and if you can walk in nature: Imagine that each footprint you leave behind provides love for anyone who follows you.

Judgement

As you go further into this journey, you will discover aspects of your past that impede your life and this discovery might cause you to be angry, hurt, disappointed, frustrated and want revenge. These are understandable emotions and valid thoughts.

Simple Steps To Managing Heavy Emotions Ⓟ1:9

First give yourself permission to experience these emotions or thoughts. Equally give yourself permission to sit with them and not respond or react to them. Bring these thoughts to mystery entering into the deepest level of silence you can achieve. State I am feeling...... and allow any words or tears to flow.

Stay in this safe place until the outpouring is settled. Ask "what can I learn from this?" Listen and stay here until you have understanding. In your imagination find where that feeling is in your body and place your hand there. Breathe in love to that place, give love a colour and swirl the colour around that place. Imagine the colour becoming richer as it absorbs all the pain or discomfort you are feeling.

When you feel that it is complete, see the light falling down into earth and all the pain being transmuted back into love. Bring in a new colour and swirl it as it fills with love. Now you understand that it is good to listen to your thoughts, to sit with them and then transmute them. When we face our hurts head on, we heal them and those thoughts will leave your body to prevent the emotions getting stuck in there to cause pain and disease. Return back to your space, drink water, stay quiet for as long as you need.

Write in your journal of your experience, the understanding, the solution and the feelings after.

Reflection

It is time now to review all that you have learned, to take time out, enter into mystery and listen to your heart. Review your journal or notes and consider the changes you have made or plan to make to your life.

This was the introduction, the very first steps toward living at your highest potential, moving forwards every day in strength and growing in power day by day. Mark this day in your diary, maybe write a letter to yourself to read at the end of the book. And congratulate yourself for all that you were able to transform and be content with what you did.

The journey of transformation is a lifelong project, keep coming back to the steps here, modify them to make them your own and teach others all that you have learned so far.

Now you have eyes to see the path before you and as we move into Drawing Back the Veil, you can enter ever deeper into your understanding of the Magic of You.

DRAWING BACK
THE VEIL

You are like a beautiful gift wrapped in a thousand layers of wrapping paper, each layer needs to be carefully unwrapped, lovingly removed to reveal the wonderful gift that you are to the world.

INTRODUCTION

To discover that you are a magical being, an extraordinary, breathtaking, magnificent being with infinite access to the miraculous is indeed amazing. Programming has prevented you from understanding this. Are you willing to debunk those old myths about yourself -not being good enough, not worthy, clumsy, stupid etc? Programming or as I call it The Veil is everything you experienced and believe, that would prevent you from knowing who you are.

Imagine if you had grown up deep in the countryside, where you connected to nature, understood the rhythms of life, of the seasons, of the moon, of the crops and harvest. This information is embedded deep within you so much so that you know when it is going to rain, you have foresight to know whether the crops will be abundant and just by looking at the tree you know which direction you're facing. You have an uncanny knack with animals both free and trained. It's as if you can whisper to them in their language and there is a great respect for each other and a deep bond.

When a visitor comes from the city, where they understand the rules, the expectations, the risks and the opportunities offered by this fast paced life, by comparison they will feel completely lost in your 'world' . They might wonder at your amazing skills, your ability to read the land, to communicate with animals and to live so freely in the air so pure. They might think you are magical, a fortune teller and be amazed.

Without judgement, both of these examples are programmes, you are programmed by family, religion, culture and the environment . Drawing back the veil is gently lifting anything that is limiting your understanding of your own magnificence. You have so much power and strength that can be used for the greater good. This power is in the very core of your being and you can peel away the layers to release all of this abundance. Opening up the door to your magnificence is like walking into Aladins cave, it is just phenomenal, breathtaking and beautiful.

Imagine for one moment that you are watching your own development from the moment you were conceived. Each cell dividing and creating your form, cell by cell you were created, you see your heart beating, your fingernails forming and you are in awe of this incredible being. It is almost unbelievable, magical, incredible and as you put your hand on your heart to feel that beat, you realise that this heart has been beating like this from before your birth. You have never seen your heart, but here it is, inside you and your programming tells you that your heart represents love.

You begin to feel the love in your heart for your family, your friends and yourself. You feel some strange sensations of power now, a sense of your magnificence, the miracle of your birth and life, a sense of calm strength lies within you and there is an urgency to know more, to understand.

You have begun the journey of unveiling the magic of you. There is so much mystery inside of you, you are a healer, a warrior, a mystic, a prophet, a musician, mathematician, a poet, an artist. Which of these roles you choose to play out in this lifetime are already programmed inside of you, your levels of success are determined by your commitment, focus and belief about yourself.

You might wonder why some people have all the luck, why some people are walking on streets paved with gold and why others, maybe more skilled, are kicking up dust. There are many factors that determine your future, the primary factor is that you already decided before you came, what you wanted to learn and experience this lifetime.

Imagine for example in your last role on earth you were a wealthy successful businessman. You made huge profits and lived a rich and powerful life. Your workers however were kept in poor and unhealthy conditions, they toiled and scraped a living from the low salary you paid them. Many died in service to you and the disparity between your life and theirs was stark.

When you transitioned from that life, you saw what you couldn't see and was ashamed. It hurt you deeply that you had treated your fellow humans so poorly and there was a desire in you to make amends. You decided that this lifetime would be a rags to rags story, that you could bring all your gifts and knowledge to people from a lowly place. When you were born you didn't have access to ta memory of this purpose and now are wondering what you are doing wrong.

This is only a story and the key learning here is to find your purpose. Wealth, abundance and longevity are of little importance compared to purpose. Are you fulfilling your purpose, do you know what it is? Are you searching for it, yearning for it and dreaming it into being?

Simple Steps To Find Your Soul Purpose

There are many ways to unlock the secrets within you: Breathing into mystery. Accessing your dream world through writing. Observing your current connections. Talking about your feelings, ideas and passions. Listening to others that inspire you. Meditating on gratitude. Removing certain words from your vocabulary: Try, Should, Must, Can't, Won't.

Purpose isn't static and has many elements, it is in itself a journey and one that you will uncover throughout the years. The more connected you are to your highest wisdom and the more layers you unveil will bring you clarity of purpose.

But there is nothing to concern yourself with as there is learning and growth with every decision you make. I will take you on a magical journey now, a journey of remembering and looking over the highlights of your past:

Hall Of Records

Imagine there is a place where every word ever spoken to or by you is recorded, encoded and stored, housed in a large space filled with all the treasures of your life. Imagine now that you can go on a journey of discovery and find yourself walking into this huge space, everything neatly catalogued, polished and treasured.

You are standing on a platform looking over the lines and lines of 'stuff'. It is a magical experience to see all these wonderful treasures of your life from here, things you imagined were lost and never to be seen again. You recognise some pieces from up here and decide to wander down to discover the pencil that you lost, your first toy, a photograph of your best friend. You spend many hours sorting through these treasures, getting lost in the memory of it and conjuring up images in your mind, conversations running through your head are playing out. All these memories are good and uplifting and you feel amazing. You wander through the years and in your memory you meet up with powerful people who transformed you and you are thrilled to recall all of this.

You move into the library of your life and sit under a soft light reading through your conversations with family members over the years and the words seem to fly off the page, you are enthralled by the experience of seeing your relationships develop and observing some of the twists and turns from both sides. You are growing in understanding and personal power through this wonderful exploration into the past. All of these memories are full of wonder and love.

Then you hear a noise and a kindly old caretaker walks in and sits and talks to you for a while, asking how you are enjoying the visit. He explains that all of these treasures and words are either from good memories or experiences that you have processed. You talk for a while and he invites you to explore another room. You follow him and find yourself outside a large door with locks on it - the sign on the door says Processing.

He explains that everything inside here are events that need attention, some stories that need processing and you agree to go in with him to work on one or two of the stories. You wait whilst he opens each lock, one by one, it seems to take a long time. The door creaks open and the light plays on the speckles of dust that leave the room. He beckons you to follow him, he smiles and walks in waving at you to follow.

You take a step into this strange room, unlike the Hall of Records or the library, there are words flying around the room, there are wisps of energy floating about, moving from one space to another. It's unlike anything you have experienced before, but you feel calm with a deep sense of knowing. The caretaker sets himself on a chair, a familiar chair that your grandfather used to sit in. You remember that you never got time to say goodbye. You look around and see memories, memories of things that you have locked away, photos of places, people, things.

You piece together some of the words floating about the room and remember who said them and how they were spoken. You speak to the caretaker about these words and the memories and he smiles reassuringly and asks you to sit with him. From somewhere he pours two mugs of steaming liquid, your favourite drink. As you sip slowly, with each sip you feel comforted and ready to sort these memories out.

The caretaker asks you if you are ready to process some memories, you feel comfortable with him and smile. He takes out an old projector and a film starts playing. On the wall, you see a grainy old film...with a scratchy sound coming from some speakers.

You see some parts of your life playing out, the words spoken and all the pieces of furniture and knick knacks in this room are there in each scene. You watch with tears streaming down your face, feeling those feelings again, wanting to hide, but knowing that there is a purpose to this. The film stops as the reel comes to its end and in the silence you have a great sense that you want to conclude this as you can see how these unprocessed memories are limiting your life today. The caretaker is talking, explaining how this is the processing room and when all the learning has been extracted from each memory and judgement ceased the treasures and the words can move into the Hall of Records and the Library.

You spend a great deal of time in this room with the caretaker, who seems familiar and you wonder if it is indeed your grandfather. You sift through memories, experiences and feelings and one by one he puts a big orange sticker on PROCESSED. You take your time and have moments of laughter as the caretaker tells you stories, there is a lightness coming over you as you let go, as you now understand why they did or said that, how you find it easy now to let that understanding turn to forgiveness and how easily you're able to set yourself and the other person free.

As you complete the last few memories and as the final sticker is adhered he presents you with a pair of glasses. The frames are rather silly, but you like them and as you're putting them on, he tells you to wear them any time you feel you are judging another or a situation and these lenses he said, will show you the truth.

Simple Steps For Reflection

Take a moment to write down your thoughts and feelings about this story. Take time to remember some of the amazing experiences that brought you to this moment and maybe pull out a photo album and spend some time enjoying a trip down memory lane.

With each image, send love and gratitude to the people and places, Find an understanding of their lives and your role in it. Speak with the people if you can or Imagine you can speak to those in spirit who have died. Gain all the learning that you can to enhance your life going forward. As you bump into those who you judge, put on a silly pair of glasses, a new lens through which to see those events and hear those words.

45

Letting Go

Part of the process of unveiling the magic of you is to undo some of the hurt by letting it go. When you take time in silence, in mystery, to process some old memories, take them slowly and ask for support from guides and mirrors.

Guides are from All that Is and may include Angels, Ascended Masters, Higher Beings, Spirit Guides and of course your highest wisdom. As you learned before, mirrors are people who play out certain roles in your life to reflect back to you all that you need to understand and guide you forward in life.

This is a simple but profound step and one that you will spend a lifetime discovering. When a memory comes to you of a person or time of your life, take a few moments to give gratitude and send love. That might be enough to move them from Processing to the Hall of Records

Surrender to your heart, let go of any thought that isn't loving you, you are precious in every way to the universe and to yourself. You have no concept of your amazingness and the magic it took to get you here. You amongst many souls were chosen to be you, the choice rested ultimately with you as to whether you would come, but the eagerness to come to earth as a human is a high prize and even for those who will only live in the womb, many would give up another opportunity to experience that again.

If you think biologically how incredible creation is, the one in a million chance of conception, the genetic connections, the risks and possibilities of life. And should you have chosen every single moment of your life before it happened, you sit now and wonder why it is so hard? How could I have chosen all of this? So far from my dream, so far from what I want. And I explain that you choose this life and create it moment by moment, the good stuff, the bad stuff, the challenges, the excitement, the joy and in all of your stories and stored memories remember you were not alone.

There is a truth about you as a soul living this life here in this body. Isn't it an amazing body? If you consider all of its possibilities and how you can train it to do the most amazing things, how it protects you, how it enables you and how it can restrict you when you become out of alignment with health.

With each experience of being out of alignment you layer your body with discomfort, each layer brings with it more discomfort and eventually you are unable to use your body the way you desire. You are here reading this because you are ready to release your fears, your stories and your experiences that led to this.

I want you to start seeing your body as this magnificent machine, loving it like it is the most precious thing on earth and in truth it is. Without this body you cannot live as you.

Will You Start Today To Love Yourself Back To The Life You Dream Of?

Treat yourself as a newborn baby, offer yourself all the love, comfort, support and care you would offer a beautiful new creation. How you choose to do this practically is 'your way', you are rewriting your story as you nurture yourself.

You can fast forward your process of learning in your imagination, remembering each moment of your life, like when you sat quietly, staring at your hands or the leaves on the trees and then think back to crawling and eventually walking - which is another miracle.

Take this slowly one tiny step at a time, make it joyful and relaxing and notice your words. The words you speak to yourself are ingrained in every cell of your body you are re-writing those cells.

Of the stories you tell yourself, can you imagine that the story is like a shirt that you put on, and with each story you put on another shirt, as the years go by you are wearing many shirts, but think about this: In the here and now would you fit into a shirt you wore at 5, 7, 11, 18 years old? They would rub, cut, chafe and all those shirts would restrict your movement and be painful. You have started the process of stripping back the layers to reveal the truth about you. How does it feel?

Setting Yourself Free

Do not fight the opportunity for freedom, because it is wrapped in different material. If freedom is offered, take it. Thousands of opportunities are presented to you every day, listen carefully, receive compliments, receive criticism, receive direction, receive kindness and receive them all equally and without judgement.

Can you choose to stretch your boundaries of thought, of spirit and body every day? Thinking outside of the thoughts that you have set for yourself, not only the negative ones, but also the neutral ones.

Think about a belief that is powerful within you: for example "when the sun goes down it will be dark". Take yourself on a journey of imagination that changes that belief - it might be a story for children with a positive message, it could be a sinister dystopian story, just play with a concept that 'argues' what you know. Have fun with this. Notice what you notice in your body, your spirit and your mind. What happened, what did you learn from this? Stretching your mind to explore different concepts will enable you to enter into this journey without restriction, limitation and in total freedom.

Has this exercise changed your mind about the dark? No, your belief remains intact, you have just explored it. As you journey through this book, all concepts, philosophies and stories you read here are to expand your mind to the possibility that all you see is not all there is.

We Conceive In Our Conscious Mind The Illusion That We Call Reality

You are programmed that seeing is believing, and to some extent this is true, you can only see what you are willing to look at, and even when you look, you might only see what you believe is possible.

This is the joy of Imagination, it creates opportunities for expansion through curiosity and opening yourself up to the supernatural. If when you were born you had knowledge of who you are and why you chose this life it would assume therefore that you had conscious thought and experience in a time before birth.

You are aware of your highest wisdom and it is in this energy body that you experienced life before life on earth, you are a soul choosing a human experience. In All that Is, you are an infinite being, this means that you are eternal, experiencing life with other souls.

We will explore this more when Walking through the Forest, but for now, know that there is so much more to this life than you are aware of today. The connections between you and all of the people in your life are uniquely designed to give each the experiences that you desire.

Imagine for now that you chose your parents as they did theirs. Sit with this thought for a while and observe this with curiosity. For many people the statement that you chose your parents comes as quite a surprise, especially if you have difficult memories of childhood. In time as you begin to change the lens through which you look at your past, this will all become very clear and unsurprising. Also imagine that each person in your life is here with the sole purpose of providing you with opportunities to experience growth and also understanding that you desire and opportunities to bring love and service to the community.

You maintain connection with your highest wisdom throughout your time on earth, this connection is there with every breath as you breathe in love through the golden thread. Taking time to make deep connections on a daily basis enables you to stay aligned with your purpose and to maintain the flow of love and healing.

Breathing With Intention

Inspire means to bring in spirit, to make that deep connection with All that Is which is love. Imagining the golden thread that connects you to your highest wisdom which is connected to All that Is, enables you to keep your focus on the breath.

Simple Steps To The Breath ⓟ2:1

Create a safe space to practise with time to focus. Enter into this practice session with curiosity and imagination and sit upright to give your lungs full capacity.

Look up to stretch your spine and then relax with your chin lifted slightly. Breathe in through your nose to maintain the balance of air and prevent hyperventilation, breathe out through your nose if it is comfortable.

Notice the temperature of the air coming in and out of your body, the natural rhythm of your breath and how your body moves with each breath. Notice any sensations of breath entering or leaving any other aspect of your body, if you find that your breath is entering an unexpected space, just allow it, watch it and maintain curiosity. Focus on the breath as it enters that space, what can you see, is there a colour there? Does that change as you breathe out? Imagine the golden light cleansing and healing that space.

Breathing Through The Heart Centre

Imagine the golden thread coming into your heart centre, breathing it in with every breath. See the golden light filling each cell of your body and envision it repairing and healing every aspect of you. Notice what you notice and imagine that you can follow the golden thread all the way back to All that Is and your highest wisdom.

Notice what you notice as you rise high up into the cosmos. Observe closely all that you imagine you can see there and communicate your intentions, desires, questions to anyone you meet.

Listen in the silence of mystery for encouragement, reassurance, direction or comfort and when you are complete: Return attention to your breath and slowly reorientate yourself to the room. Write in your journal: recording your experiences, knowing that you can always travel into All that Is whenever you wish to expand your knowledge and wisdom.

Interpreting The Messages

When speaking with your guides there is a need to listen without judgement, with the lens of curiosity and truth. Over time you will begin to trust the messages you hear. When you receive direction in response to a powerful question, sit with it, write about it, speak to trusted friends, review and assess and do not act upon it until you have built a trust in your own skills of interpretation.

Over the years you will grow in intuitive skills and will be able to see whether the direction is in any way contaminated by your own desires or fears. This is why we need each other, why we need to ensure that we are not working alone and why we need to learn from each other.

LENS AND FILTERS

I have spoken about the lens through which you look at life. The lens is determined by your life experience, your culture, education and belief system. If you have been hurt by a man, you might see all men through the same lens. If a boy with straw coloured hair and glasses beat you up as a child, when you see a boy with straw coloured hair and glasses you might be triggered by those memories and expect the same from this new child. And if you had a girlfriend who cheated and lied to you, all girls might be viewed in this light.

On the journey of transformation, all of the steps outlined in this book will lead you towards the lens of love. The opposing lens is fear. Fear is shorthand for everything that is a symptom of the experience you absorbed into your being, it is everything that is not love.

The lens of love enables you to respond, rather than react, you will use this lens throughout the book to challenge and change the stories that brought you to this point in your life. You will also skill yourself to be able to recognise when you have swapped out to the lens of fear and this will guide you on the path of transformation.

Please go at your own pace, the book cannot determine your needs and it took a great deal of time to get you to this moment, and if it takes a year or more to go through the stages of the book, then that is alright. Remember Everything is in Perfect Order.

How you view your life today and the experiences you have had, will radically change if you take time to get comfortable. If an exercise feels uncomfortable and out of alignment with where you are today, ignore it, go to the next step and come back to it another day.

Other People's Opinions

How do you filter other people's opinions of you, their attitude towards you and the language they use against you without losing your power?

Ask yourself: do you believe what they are saying?

Yes: What evidence is there to prove that? Who told you that this was true? Who or what situation confirmed it? Is this something other people think about you? Is there something you can do about this? Do you want to take action to change? Bring this to Mystery

No: Is there any evidence that could be found to prove this to be true? Is that evidence outdated - for example that was when you were an angsty teenager? Does the person have an issue with you? What lens are they looking at you through? Is it the lens of Love or Fear? Is there anything can you say or do to support the accuser to review their charge? Is it time to walk away? Bring this to mystery

When you step back from others' opinions, the need to retaliate or enter into drama and conflict is removed. You have made a decision to breathe and to mindfully consider the accusation. This will put the other on the back foot and allow you time to consider your response. For simplicity and to give yourself time. Thank them for sharing their opinion and ask for time to consider their accusation or just walk away.

The opinions of others are more about them than you. They have chosen the lens of fear and have stepped away from love. You will begin to recognise when you put on the Lens of Fear which causes you to compare yourself and judge others. Over time the need to share your internal thoughts and judgements will be replaced with giving people permission to live as they wish.

Discernment

I understand discernment to be a state of knowing and being alert to the markers that guide this knowledge. It is recognising the truth in all that you hear and see. If you are observing a pattern of behaviour in another or yourself, being able to discern whether this is born out of love or fear, will enable you to make the necessary changes to your life to either protect or transform yourself.

When there is recognition that the root of presenting behaviour, was created in a fearful often traumatic event and that the person is now using the lens of fear to perceive and act out in life. Then judgement is suspended. At this stage in your journey of transformation, it will suffice to practise being comfortable and easy about discerning both yours and others behaviours in this way.

Simple Steps To Discernment Of Others

Take off the judge's wig, as wearing it is always a choice. Get comfortable with observing from a distance, remember, this is not personal, this is about them.Check your emotions and reactions, allow them, acknowledge them, sit with them and get comfortable with them.

Observe behaviours and make a mental note of what you are seeing, observe body language: are they closed down or explosive or something else? Engage fully in active listening, observe the tone and timbre of their voice, the language and descriptors used and learn to read between the lines as often what is not said is more powerful and meaningful than what is said. If you are able: Imagine the person in a ball of golden light and fill them with love, keep your energy relaxed and calm, speak slowly and quietly and maintain eye contact. Keep your face neutral and relaxed and exit the exchange as soon as you can.

Reflect on all you have observed and learned.

If You Are A Sensitive Person

Breathe in the beauty of everyday whatever is occurring, whatever is happening, wherever you are and whatever you are doing, breathe in the beauty of that day. What does this actually mean? How do you breathe in the beauty in the midst of chaos? How do you breathe in the beauty in the midst of discord? How do you breathe in the beauty when you're out of alignment with beauty?

When you breathe with the intention of finding beauty, your awareness peaks. Every day you are breathing in the energies around you, if you are sensitive you will be picking up everything and this is why you might feel uncomfortable. You will find that your energy shifts in certain places or when you are watching certain things on the screen, being in crowds and in shopping centres. There may be times if you are highly sensitive where you might just feel that you are contaminated by everything.

Let me explain the energies in the air: Air is filled with love but also the vibration of words, thoughts, fears, behaviours and memory. When you are on a personal & spiritual quest, it's absolutely imperative that you create a filter and that you use your filter of intuition to decide what is for your highest potential and what is not.

I want to talk to you about how you create this filter: If we look at your physiology, you have a brain that tells you this and that and you have to decide whether you want this or that. You make those decisions based on who you are, your culture and education. These decisions will take you down known and unknown paths and might be exactly the place you need to be. However if you are living a life of freedom, then you need the filter of intuition, which once connected with your highest wisdom will guide you down often unknown paths towards your highest potential and purpose.

Discerning right or wrong and this or that is in the domain not of the mind but of the heart centre, the connection to your highest wisdom. Making that connection in order that you can discern and decide the right way forward is completely necessary on the journey of awakening to your magnificence.

As you engage in deeper levels of curiosity and imagination, the filter of intuition will change your perception of reality and provide you with a new narrative. How you choose to communicate all that you are seeing and feeling will depend on how grounded you are in your truth and confident you are with your beliefs.

Building a powerful relationship with your intuition and guidance from your highest wisdom will guard against going down the wrong path and enable you to search out your purpose without being tossed from one idea to another. It will also support you to communicate the changes you are experiencing without judgement or feelings of superiority.

Take some time out now to sit and contemplate your own journey to date: How your breathing has changed, your ability to enter into mystery, how you feel physically, your relationships, your path, your purpose, perception of life without judgement and an ability to see beauty.

Meditation For Discernment
℗2:2

Gently put your hand on your heart and breathe in through your heart space, breathing love through the golden thread. Bring before you the faces of people or things that you love and connect deeply with them.

Smile and know that you are completely safe. State the dilemma, the this or that and the direction you desire. Invite your guides to support your journey.

Ask to see the next step before you on this path, if you are a visual person ask for a visual, if you are an intellectual person ask for a metaphor and if you're a mathematician ask for an equation. Ask your guides to bring before you over the next few days a sign or symbol that you will understand and let go of the question and stay with your breath for as long as you can. You

Then gently bring your awareness back to the space. Express your gratitude for the support, knowing that the answer will come and go about your day being observant and reflective. When the symbol is shown to you, take the symbol however it comes and write it down or draw it.

Bring your awareness to any feelings present in you, the thoughts in your mind and gain a real sense of who you are, a real sense of your power, your purpose and how you need to move forward.

The more you practice with smaller questions the greater the power of discernment will be within you, and remember even if you go down a cul-de-sac you will still have many more learning experiences.

Do not expect that everybody will do this process the same because you are unique, you are wired differently than everybody else and your vibrational frequency is different than everybody else's in this moment and will be different with each meditation for discernment, so how you do this has to be as unique as you are.

Judgement

We all make judgments, for example: 'I think it is odd that the majority of people on earth are disconnected from the land', although of course this is not true of all, it is a judgement that is unhelpful. The moment we enter into judgement we must recognise that this is a reflection of an area in our life in need of healing. In All that Is there is no judgement, everything is seen as a valuable lesson. Each event or experience is reviewed objectively, listened to and commented on as valuable learning for all.

As a collective, we need to listen to the stories people share with us, learning how they perceive and respond to the world and then to examine their personal created belief system. When it goes against the collective accepted norm, pay attention, open your eyes and see as if for the first time, become as a child in complete innocence, take everything as if it is the most fascinating thing you have ever heard.

Listen with your heart to the young members of your community, listen until your heart is overjoyed by their creativity, their understanding, their forward movements. Yes they may be challenging but find yourself in deference to these new and wonderful ideas. If you find resistance then know that it is about you and not about them and seek your own healing.

When I was in Egypt, the young were challenging, they wanted to see new and different things than those we had created. They didn't agree with the current systems and argued passionately for new rules and models of living. They saw new ways of doing things, they spent their lives dreaming and acting, they played in the dirt, they built castles in the air, they enacted new ways of being and they were charming. Where would the world be now if the older generations had stopped all of their experiments? Still playing in the dirt? And look where you are now, with your technology, transport, education and acceptance of other belief systems, in constant flow and transformation.

Defining Purpose

You are here for one purpose and that is to expand into the human being that you desired and chose to be. In order that you can do this you have to make some decisions which may be in conflict with parental guidance and parental decisions that they made on your behalf. You might even disagree with some of the systems and processes that your parents and your community followed. You might choose to go against their political and religious beliefs and you may choose not conform to the societal norms of the day.

How you choose to live as an adult is your choice and you are not here to be moulded into a carbon copy of your parents, siblings, friends, family or community.

You are here to expand, to create and to be a powerful instrument of change in this world. In the process of life you will meet challenges again and again. There is no doubt that these challenges are possibly the most powerful experiences of expansion. Yet in human experience they can be overwhelming and sometimes they can close down any possibility of expansion.

When facing these challenges, for example when people argue against your beliefs, you might make the decision to conform because you feel it is too difficult to maintain your position. As you grow through life, there may be a feeling that there is something missing, that there is more to life than you are living and you might look upon others who've achieved your dream and purpose with great jealousy. This might lead to regret and anger towards those who put you down and stymie your ability to move forwards but it is never too late and now your dream might be realised.

Life circumstances may disable your ability to be completely free, yet if you work on the principle that Everything is in Perfect Order, then you can view your life as an opportunity to express yourself in new and interesting ways. Your reality is a construct of the mind and if you choose to see it as a prison - then you will feel trapped, conversely see it as an adventure and new opportunities will come into your life. Bring imagination and curiosity into every situation you find yourself in and discover new and exciting ways to fulfil your dreams.

To live the life that you dream, you must first live the dream in your imagination. For example if your dream is to travel: because you want to expand your knowledge of different cultures and different countries and explore what it might feel like to be in the presence of these people, to taste the cuisine and understand their lifestyle, culture, architecture and belief systems. Yet you are in a position where you cannot afford to travel or you haven't got the physical capacity or have commitments that prevent you. This is when you can look for alternate ways to live your dream by studying and exploring from your home and broadening your knowledge.

When I was a young person in Egypt, I couldn't have dreamt of all the things that you dream of now. Life beyond our community was outside of our understanding and there was a deep contentment and acceptance of our lot. We knew our place and enjoyed our lives and life was in many ways simple. Although we didn't speak of gratitude, we were grateful and fulfilled. As you come to an understanding and realisation of the dream which may or may not be more than the seeds of your purpose, hone it down so that you can find ways to fulfil it.

If your dream is about defining yourself and projecting that image: Fashion is a way of exploring your individuality: Learn how to make clothes or design clothes of your own. You may wish to express your individuality in a certain hairstyle: Create that style yourself and experiment. If it is to serve others in a certain way: Gain knowledge and skills to enable you and then take action. If it is to write, draw, paint, sculpt or create: Start today, every day building your knowledge,skills and abilities.

If when you come to the end of your life you have not managed to fulfil your dreams do not be upset, do not beat yourself up, do not feel that you have failed because you haven't. Even the experience of not fulfilling your dreams creates expansion because for some people they come here willingly to not achieve their dreams to experience all the emotions that disappointment creates.

The Power Of Saying No

There were times when I was expected to behave in certain ways and make choices that I didn't agree with, I am sure you have found the same in your lives. Consider all the choices you have made for others, for your faith, religion, culture, parents, education, friends and lovers that went against your own intuitive desires and beliefs. Review two or three of those experiences, not to get caught up in the story, but to extract all the learning from them.

Each experience is valuable, if you view it without judgement and with a lens of curiosity and enquiry. Then, when you have learned all there is to learn from those two or three experiences. Turn the learnings into statements that you can tell yourself next time you are asked to do something you don't agree with.

There is great value in exploring stories that might have defined your life and stories that people hold you in. For example if you were a wayward child who was full of enquiry and experimentation, followed your own path and then when you found it, turned it into a successful life. Those who knew you as a wayward child might still hold those stories of you today despite your obvious success.

Managing others' views of you is your responsibility. You have the power to choose whether their view has validity and whether you will act upon it or not. Every opportunity presented is an opportunity to decide which direction you want to go and who you want to carry with you. Your response and reactions are indicators of your personal power and as you recognise the biological response that leads you to act in certain ways, the speedier your transformation will be.

Do not expect to magically change every aspect of your life all at once. You are aiming to transform your life with the least disruption possible. Depending where you are on your spiritual path will determine the pace you are comfortable to take. Taking one step at a time is vital to maintain your equilibrium and not rock your world off kilter. Making powerful choices is a perfect place to start, but first build the foundations that you need to start building this new spiritual life.

I started small, I was discreet and did not make a show to the world, I was happy to go undercover to learn my trade, to truly help people heal and to work with the dying and lost souls. This took many years of work before I was recognised and then I was able to truly shine bright. I invite you to take the simple steps in this book slowly. I also invite you to find your tribe of people at different stages of their personal and spiritual development in order that you can learn and share your own experiences and questions.

I will always tell you that there is no wrong way, and even if you find that you have made mistakes, extract the learning from them and be grateful. If the mistake involved another, then apologise to them and thank them for the learning it offered you.

Simple Steps To Determine Response To A Request

First check the lens you are using (seeing), then check the filter you are using (hearing), listen to the words formed in the question. Observe the body language of the person asking. Repeat the request back for clarification then ask what time scale they need for your answer. If it is immediate, decline and say you cannot do this without consideration.

Write the question down in your journal and bring your breath to focus and observe your biological responses to this question. It is known now that excitement and anxiety feel the same so measure well. Allow a stream of writing without correcting or reading, allowing words to flow and if you get stuck, rewrite the question. You will know when you are complete, there will be a pause in you and you might notice your body starts to feel different and your mind becomes clearer.

Stop writing, sit back, close your eyes. Pull before you the face of someone you love and who loves you, who offers a mirror of encouragement. Allow your breath to guide you into a place of calm and call in your guides and explain the question. Tell them the answer you are leaning towards and then listen for their guidance: This might be a voice in your head or a sense in your heart. Speak out the answer you have understood and feel what that feels like saying Yes or No

and once again check biological reactions. This might seem like a long winded way to make a decision, remember you are creating new patterns of awareness and allowing your life to be heart centred rather than head centred. The more you practice the less time this will take

Saying Yes Or No

Having completed a process of heart centred decision making you can make contact with the person to deliver your answer. Without judgement the answer is clear and you are not to be swayed, although you might have concluded that there is a middle ground.

When meeting with the person, if the answer is not what they were expecting, you need to be cautious of your language, the way you present your decision, as you will not want to damage either yourself or them.

Simple Steps To Declining The Request

Bring the person to mind and imagine them in a ball of light. Fill that ball of light with love and speak with authority explaining that you have taken time to make a decision and understand that they will be disappointed but you hope they will listen to your reasons. Then calmly explain the reasons why you are declining and if you have a middle ground offer, make it here. Whilst you are talking, observe the person and fill your heart with love for them.

Very often the veil we hide behind is one of compliance, making decisions that are self-limiting and damaging, rather than life enhancing and self loving. Even if you played these steps out only in your mind, you will have made a powerful step forwards in your transformation.

Conflict

In a roundabout way we've actually explored conflict. As conflict more often than not is within your own minds and is a construct of our fears. When we find ourselves in conflict with other people, we must take this as an opportunity for growth.

Start by going inwards to find your core strength, beliefs and feelings in order that you can communicate your position with power. If you discover unhealed aspects of yourself, then find your path to healing. Then consider the other person, what led them to their thoughts and beliefs and feelings? Is it cultural, religious, born through experience, unhealed trauma? Then determine the outcome you want from the exchange.

There is nothing more beautiful than having different views and being able to share without fear of damage to the relationship. There is no right or wrong, there are only different perspectives. Can you allow other people to have different views than yours?

Differing views can offer the greatest opportunity for creativity and expansion. For example: Imagine if you were charged with the responsibility of creating a new form of transport. You would gather a team of experts around you and engage in healthy debate to draw out the most creative, sustainable and viable design. Each person would play their role in that design, from technical experts right through to design expertise. Together you would create a functional and beautiful vehicle and all of your different viewpoints, even the ones that were rejected are responsible for the final outcome.

Life on earth can be viewed like this example, you are responsible for expansion and development of new ideas and ways of being. The youth of each generation are here to ensure that old ways are transformed into new and exciting models of living and it is important to not hold too tightly to your beliefs today.

With this concept and understanding of expansion, can you now see that conflict can be viewed as a great opportunity for growth? Where you cannot find agreement or concord, are you willing to agree to differ without losing your relationship?

Meditation For Concord   ℗2:3

Before you begin this meditation, prepare yourself by agreeing on a time and space where you will give yourself permission to go deeper into mystery. Ensure that you are at the peak of health, having eaten well, slept well and have spent time in nature to create a sense of balance and harmony within you. When you are ready to honour yourself with this time, create a space that is both beautiful, aromatic and calm.

For this meditation, sit upright, supported and comfortable. Focus on your breath, breathing out in a long sigh as you release any tension or thoughts that are concerning you. Let the inbreath be full into your belly and out breath be long and releasing.

On the outbreath, visualise all of your stress, strain, discomfort leaving your body in wisps of coloured energy. Imagine that each cell of your body is releasing anything that doesn't serve you, that limits you, that holds you back from a life of creativity, curiosity and peace.

When the wisps of energy turn golden then you know that you are connected through the golden thread to the source of love. Now pull in the radiant golden light from earth up into your spine and out of your head in a shower of love. In this taurus of golden light you are now free to go deeper into mystery.

Imagine you can pick out one sparkle of golden light in front of you, watch it as it moves around, stay focussed on it as your body relaxes as the movement helps you drift deeper into a state of nothingness. The sparkle of golden light becomes all consuming as you sit, losing for this moment your connection with your beingness, your separateness.

Imagine you are merging with the energies of earth and All that Is, that you are becoming one with everything you know and do not yet know and that you are now this beautiful sparkle of golden light.

As you drift into the purity of this sparkle, moving at

will, rising, falling, swooping, hovering, you feel the power within, the sense of oneness and connectedness to all other sparkles of light around you.

The peace that passes all understanding, is here now, in this moment and you exhale the beauty of it and breathe in the love and understanding of the whole of creation. Stay here for as long as you need to fully engage in presence and when you are ready, bring that beautiful sparkle of light and place it in your heart, watch it cleanse and heal your body and move up into your mind and cleanse and heal your thoughts and then into your spine to strengthen and support you, and into your feet to guide you and into your arms and hands to embrace you.

Bring yourself back into the present, into your being and your life.

Reflect in your journal to gain the greatest understanding from this place of deep mystery and love.

LOVE

Love is a much greater force than you know, it is the very essence of life - it permeates everything and when you touch its magic, you cannot un-touch it. You make a connection to love through mystery, your time of silence, unhurried connection to All that Is. Love is not a tangible thing, it's a deep, incredibly powerful experience. You are born of love, you are love, you embody love and when I speak of All that is and your highest wisdom, I speak of you.

A growing baby in the womb has an umbilical cord through which all the nutrients it needs to grow are fed by its mother. It also has a golden thread that connects it to All that Is through its highest wisdom. Imagine that this golden thread is where all the knowledge, wisdom and love from All that Is, is accessed. On the path to enlightenment the stronger this connection through the golden thread, the deeper the understanding of love.

The path to enlightenment is hidden behind the veil, the veil is many layered: the stories, the experiences and the memories which you hold tight to. The lens through which you view life is coloured by these experiences and may distort your access to pure essence love. As you break through these layers, you reveal the true magic of you. The miracle of your creation and the true reason why you are here on earth at this time.

A Simple Practice

Deepening the connection with your highest wisdom requires a journey, a daily exploration into your thoughts, dreams and goals. It also takes unwrapping the binds that have restricted you since the events that impacted you

It is true that these events happened but is this the truth? Is the story you tell, one of hope and a positive future or is it one of woe and despair, loss and grief? Wrapping yourself in the past is like wrapping yourself in decaying materials which only serve to stifle growth, rather than extracting the learning from past experiences to feed your future. The same way that the nutrients from decaying material in the forest are used to maintain the balance of life and support new growth. Can you look at your stories in the same way?

Your stories, your experiences led you to where you are today. You wouldn't be who you are as a physical being without those stories. All the people you have met along the way, the opportunities you chose for forward movement. Your geography, employment, volunteering, interest groups and training choices are all because of the past. Where is the past? How relevant is it to you today? How does reliving the past move you closer to your goals?

One very simple way to focus on this is to write: to explore your thoughts and write about them. Day by day you will uncover your magic as you put closure to ideas, beliefs and stories that have held you prisoner. Create a rhythm to this, decide when and where you will write and how long you will write for, this is catharsis, no need for fancy journals - this is a different process. Entering into the magic of you, to find that deep and wonderful connection to ALL that Is will become easier and lighter with this process.

A simple way to review your story is to look for the positives, finding the gems of learning and seeing how it led you to now and being thankful.

Gratitude

There is a power in gratitude that cannot be underestimated, the act of being thankful and expressing those thoughts is one of the keys to raising your vibration to the highest level.

The higher the vibration you can reach, the more you will create a life in flow. If you want to live a life in flow, to create ease, to manage stress and strains and natural events with calm and strength then gratitude is a practice that will 'grease the path'

It is very easy to think about what is wrong, out of whack, out of alignment, to make judgements, to bemoan life circumstances. Gratitude will not change what is, but it will change how you view it.

Consider one area of your life that you need to transform, let us begin for the purposes of this exercise with considering your health. Maybe you want to be fitter, stronger, more mobile, in less pain, slimmer or heavier. All of these are possible but the transformation will at first take place in the mind. Changing your mind about your body will guide you to healthier choices and actions. Gratitude, although a spiritual practice actually changes the way you perceive and think about everything including your health.

Simple Steps To Gratitude

Adopt a routine that works for you and make a commitment and stick to it.

For example: Before you get out of bed: Name three things or people you are grateful for. It's ok to repeat these, but have fun with this and maybe use alliteration: "I'm grateful for Amazing Apples" And when you eat that apple later - remember that this fruit is amazing and smile.

During your shower or bath as you are washing your body say: I'm so grateful for my spine that keeps me strong every day. I'm grateful for my feet and all the miles they have carried me. I'm grateful for my arms that are strong enough to carry heavy weights and gentle enough to carry a baby. And as you dry or apply cream continue with your gratitude

When you get in your vehicle, be grateful for the freedom it provides for you. When you are with your family, friends, colleagues: Look upon them with curiosity and smile, tell them how much you value them and thank them for all they give to you.

When you are eating food or drinking: Give thanks for the farmers who planted & harvested the crops. Give thanks for the drivers who carried the crops. Give thanks for the people who processed the crops and prepared them for sale. Give thanks for the people who sold the products. And give thanks for the person who prepared your food.

When you are in nature: Give thanks for the beauty, the majesty and abundance of creation and really begin to notice everything around you. As you find your own, natural and easy way of being grateful, you will notice that the lens through which you see life is changing. You are becoming mindful and thoughtful, noticing life and people around you that may have been a blur on your screen of life.

Mystery

Entering into mystery requires practice and rhythm, allowing yourself time to 'flow' or float gently on the waters of life. Choose a time and place where you can enter into silence, using your breath to calm and bring your intention to the primary thoughts or concerns that you have written about. Allow the silence to wrap you in safety and comfort whilst your thoughts journey to All that Is and return through the golden thread transmuted into understanding and love.

Breathe in the love from All that Is and sit with love until you are in surrender to the learning. If there is a need to set free another person involved in the event, breathe out the light of love you are receiving and send it to them, imagine them floating into the distance wrapped in the light of love.

Then bring yourself back to the room, drink water, stretch, put your hands on your heart, feel the connection to spirit flooding through you and then get on with your day.

Every day take off more layers of conditioning to reveal your magnificence and seek out your tribe to grow together through life challenges.

WANDERING THROUGH THE FOREST

I am wanting to show people how to live harmoniously with others - to challenge them to step back from their thoughts and a need to be right. I want them to know that they are a small cog in the wheel of life and their role is vital and they do not need to vie for superiority.

INTRODUCTION

You are not alone, you are deeply connected to All that Is in the universe, there is nothing that separates you beyond your mind. As you journey in the forest you will uncover more layers of the magic or magnificence of you and learn new ways to navigate the human experience.

We can learn a great deal through metaphors, explore possibilities that might not be easily represented by actual events. Using the metaphor of a forest, we can explore connections, to see how you are connected to everything around you, how you are interdependent with Earth and with all its inhabitants.How when we choose to live and work, in community, in connection with people, we can be influenced and influence others.

When I lived in Egypt, I was integral to the community, although I was not equal to the people, I walked among them, I knew them by name, I heard their cries, I understood their joys and their plights. I returned to my home but spent many hours in the community, I fed those who had nothing whilst they found their power again to live independently. It is my heartfelt desire that as you journey through these pages, you will remember your power and live your life from today transformed by your experience and own magnificence.

You have explored the beginnings of your purpose, but in this stage we are looking at your intrinsic qualities. Those qualities that are not moveable, that you would stand by irrespective of external influence or demand. Many of these qualities are being revealed as you unveil the old stories and discover your true unlimited nature. The story of you is as individual, unique and remarkable as it is with all those you meet up with on your path. You are special, valued, important and loved and in order to live in harmony with the world, these are the principles that will lead you to that truth.

You are special: there is only one person in the whole of earth that is like you and that is you. Your infinite being expressed in this body, in this culture, in this timeline, with all the experiences you have had, have created you. You are unique, the only one of your kind and as you travel along life's journey you will continue to create life in your special way.

You are valued: you might wonder 'who values me'?   Can you imagine the workings of an analogue watch, a tiny watch with golden numbers. When you open it you see the workings, the tiniest cogs and screws and wheels you have ever seen and you wonder how anything so exquisite can be so small and function so smoothly. In the whole of the cosmos, you are as small as the tiniest cog in this watch and you know that it would not work without you.

Everyone on earth is playing their part, they are a screw, a cog, a wheel or maybe a spring. They have all agreed to the role they will play to make the watch work or maybe Planet Earth evolve harmoniously. Whatever role you agreed to, you will fulfil and you will do this in this unique and special expression in physical form known by the world as you.

This makes sense now why you are important, why you are alive at this time, why you have chosen the path you are choosing today and the people, culture and geography you find yourself in. You might ask if you have freewill to ignore your call or do something different and wonder what will happen to the 'timepiece' if you don't honour your agreements?

This is the call of your spirit, your soul energy and your love. In the event that you get lost on your path, your guides, your loved ones will encourage you back onto the path. You are always loved towards making **healthy and positive choices for your life, but in the event that you reject** the call and live a completely different life, there will be no judgement as all life experience moves the planet forwards. The 'metaphorical timepiece' will adapt to fill the gap.

You are loved: each cell in your body is made from love and is filled with love. Each breath you take is filled with love and the water and food you eat is filled with love. Earth radiates love and your soul radiates the golden light of love through the golden thread and you cannot escape it. You are love.

When you feel unloved you are referring to the emotion of love, which is a completely different topic we will discuss later. You are love. Within your daily practice of filling yourself with the radiant golden light from earth and through the golden thread, you are infusing yourself, this will work with you to restore balance and calm in your life, your body and your mind.

As you unveil the beautiful mystery of you and release the layers of life that have kept you in hiding, you will be more and more aware that you are not only Loved but you actually are love. The need for others' approval and affirmation will reduce and you will begin to know the power of you and how to use that power within you to navigate the journey of life.

A Single Step   Ⓟ3:1

Create a space in your life to embrace your imagination, first go into mystery through the breath and then read slowly painting the images in your mind as the words come to life on the page.

The trees are looming overhead, with their heavy branches, glistening sunshine is falling upon your head and you have a lightness of step as you travel through the moist and rich land, it has been dry so you are comfortable and don't need to focus on your path except for the branches that have fallen and the roots that have stretched out to touch their family.

Here the air is clear, the magic is tangible, you know

that there are multiple life forms, from microscopic spores to full grown trees. The diversity of this forest is rich and welcoming and there's a sense of belonging. Drink in this majesty for a moment, understand how you belong here, although you are neither a spore or a tree - you are a human being sharing this earth with these trees these spores yet connected and evolving in some way. The fruits of the earth, the air , sunlight, moisture are all shared , all dependent on each other.

As you take a moment of quiet stillness, take this time to touch a tree, to feel its bark, the textures, the growth from within that caused the patterns, and with both palms touch the tree and send it love from your heart. Form a symbiotic relationship with the tree, to share in this magical moment of now, to reach into the world the tree has created around it, see if you can sense its role here, it's position in this community, listen to it's stories and receive it's love, for you are in this moment as a tree - welcomed into the community. Speak to it, sharing your story and feel for one moment that these tree branches are hugging you, comforting and reassuring you. Allow this silent exchange to heal you and imagine the energy fizzing through the tree - pulling in the sunlight from above and the deep moisture from the ground in an infinite flow and as you connect to the tree, allow yourself to meld with it to be a part of this flow.

Bring to mind all of the areas of weakness you have in your body and mind and allow this flow to cleanse and heal you. Rest deeply in this exchange, without hurry or desire to move, stay as long as you can, knowing that the love of the forest is coming through you from all the life here. Harmony feels like this, without ego, without hurry, without fear. This is community, this is what you seek, this is how to do it - this is how it is in All that Is, the essence of all with its sole purpose to cleanse, to heal, to love.

Mycelium The Infinite Network Below Our Feet

The language of trees is a mystery except to those who study them and understand their nature, the indigenous people who live in the land and can read each forest track like you are reading this book. Sit for a while in the middle of a forest, in silence, observing, listening, imagining and you will begin to see the elements working seamlessly in harmony with all.

Imagine now your feet have roots growing from them, with every breath they magically grow and work their way into the ground, through the top soil and deeper into the land, imagine that you can feel the roots as they force their way, splitting and growing and moving ever forwards. Notice how the energy is rising through the roots into your whole being - if you can't, just imagine it, pretend. Feel your connection to the land and then out of the blue as you are focussed on your body another sensation bolts through you. You immediately alter your attention to the roots and find that one tip of root has connected with another, you cannot clearly see what sort of root it is, but there are many fine roots and as you follow them upwards towards the forest floor you see a fungi growing on an old tree stump.

Now you are connected to the fungi, and you search around the ground and see the roots of the old stump, still alive, still vibrant and the pulsing energy flowing through the stump and the fungi together creating energetic rhythms and you are connected to them both. You feel overwhelmed to be a part of this forest and you begin to see how your humanity is dependent on all creation here in the forest. That you are far from separate, you are an integral part of the flora and fauna of this beautiful forest which is a part of the whole of Earth. You feel humbled, connected and at peace.

You Are Called To Let Your Light Shine

As the mycelium covers the earth creating a network of

communication and passing along healing energies and information, so too lightworkers are connected. Imagine the globe with light sticks stretching out into the sky, pillars of lights all over the world. There was a time not long ago when there were very few light pillars and some were dimmed. As the earth is vibrating at a higher level and more people are waking up to the mystery and magic of life, divesting themselves of the 'old stories' there are more and more pillars of light shining across the globe.

As a lightworker, know that when you pull in the golden light from the universe you shine to all the world and it's a beautiful sight. The more powerful you become the brighter the light and more people will wake up as they are drawn to you like a magnet. The more people who become aware of their magnificence, the higher the vibration of the planet and the golden light will shine greater and attract more people.

WAKING UP

Some might still wonder what this means, it means making a deep and real connection to that inner being, the magic and mystery of your energetic body, the vehicle through which you are connected to All that Is.

An acorn when it falls to the ground has the heart of the oak inside its shell. The mother tree will support its life but will not let all the acorns grow into trees as there must be order to the forest. The heart of you is energetic source energy, your spirit, your divine nature, your connection to All that Is. The trunk is your body, the vehicle in which you travel this land, without which there is no life.

You connected with a tree stump, and discovered that its roots were still alive and transforming the life of the forest, giving shelter to the fungi and a seat for the passers by. Never underestimate the power of creation, even those who you might dismiss. Make that connection with all those you are drawn to, transform them just by linking your roots together.

Distraction From Your Path

There are always places you must be, people you must see and tasks that need completing. The demands on you are great and the more you are present in life, the greater the demands. How do you keep focus and not stray off your path?

You are full of routine and are by nature a routine person, even in your chaos there will be repetitive patterns that you follow. Patterns give you structure and security, they help you position yourself in the world and take action where necessary. When you are going through hard and difficult times, either internal or external, these patterns are disrupted. But if you consider your 'routines' , the way you clean your teeth, and the way you make your morning drink etc these will remain. The reason they will remain is because they are automatic, you are on autopilot. These patterns are so well trodden like animal tracks in the forest and they are very hard to change. Finding time for you is not difficult if you look at these automatic habits. Piggy back onto these to ensure that you can maintain your focus.

A Simple Exercise

Write a list of all repetitive patterns of behaviour that you perform on autopilot like brushing your teeth, showering, boiling a kettle.

Write a list of personal development practices you want to embed in your daily routine in order that they become a habit. Match the two lists together as best you can then practice and have fun with the new patterns you are creating in your day.

It might be that you choose to practice breathwork whilst the kettle is boiling. Gratitude, between the morning alarm and getting up. Meditation before you turn off the light at night. Once you have these patterns well embedded in your daily routine, they will remain.

When a practice requires dedicated focus and time: review your life choices, those that are non-negotiable and those that are. Make decisions based on the level of disruption and impact your practice will have upon others lives.

You might choose to get up an hour earlier, make preparations for the morning before you retire. You might cancel a subscription or group you attend and for a period of time decline invitations that are out of alignment with your practice and process. If you maintain your practice or process regularly then on holidays or sick days, you can just manage what you are able without guilt.

Perception

Your view of life is unique to you and based upon the lens you are looking through and all of the experiences that bear similarity. Variances in perception provide opportunity for creative force and evolution of ideas and development. Holding differing views with trusted people with the lens of curiosity and love will bring forward great learning and further bonding between you.

Exploring opposing views can be rife with difficulty if there is a lack of respect and honour for the other person. On the path to transformation, you will meet up with these wonderful opportunities to assist your growth. When you find that your views oppose others and you have a personal need for validation this can throw you off balance. These experiences are an excellent training ground and how you move forward from here will determine the ease of your path.

Simple Steps

Thank the person for sharing their views and say you find them interesting. Tell them you have quite different ideas and would really value an opportunity to consider these alternative views and maybe return to discuss them at another time.

When you have time to process these thoughts, sit down and consider the exchange, maybe write down what you heard and what you understood. Write about the feelings you experienced: Did you feel: Challenged, Put down, Ridiculed, Angry, Vulnerable or something else?

Breathe into the feelings and sit with them for a while. Ask your guides and your highest potential if there is any learning or action you need to take in regards to the root of those feelings. If so, take to mystery and explore, otherwise, learn all you can about the opposing view.

Consider what lens and experience might have brought the other to this opinion. Hold a private debate with yourself: Ask yourself - 'what if it's true'. Argue for the other person's opinion, really 'sell the idea to yourself'. When you are spent, think about your own personal opinion and how you are feeling now?

The purpose of these simple steps is to find 'neutral'. This means that you are of no opinion about others opinions. The more you practise this, the easier you will find that the opinions of others have no impact on you. You can use these ideas to support you if you find them useful: Everyone is doing the best they can with the resources they have and Everything is in Perfect Order.

Validation

As a child, you sought permission and validation because you were learning the art of being human. Maybe gaining praise when you first crawled and took the first step. When you smiled others smiled back. You learned by the reactions of others whether you were good or bad.

As an adult, opportunities for validation reduce, if your need for validation remains important then, you will be sorely disappointed if you seek it outside of yourself.

Seek validation within:
Set your benchmark for achievement, it doesn't matter if this is high or low in the world's eyes. Make a commitment to yourself to attain the prize you award yourself and when you achieve: Celebrate! Take yourself on a date, spoil yourself, have fun and create space for you to shine. Pat yourself on the back and know that you have won. Keep setting yourself small steps towards the life you dream of, so that you can gain the validation you need.

You will notice confidence growing within as you build this core strength. Others will notice the changes in you too, as they will see you as less needy as after all you are building strength and confidence in yourself.

It's not fair: Do you still feel this? This is a hangover from childhood that needs attention in the adult world. When you were young, battling with your siblings and peers for authority, displays of strength or accomplishments, you measured yourself against others. It may be that they had the exact same bicycle you wanted but couldn't have. It may be that they had beautiful curly long hair and yours was straight. The need to be equal is understandable but not realistic within the adult world.

One of the biggest lies that you are told is that you are separate - you are not. There is a balance on earth and this is necessary for growth. There are those who can and those who can't as there are those who have and those who have not.

The wonderful mixture and diversity of humans is not a mistake. As cells in each part of your body are different, so are people in your world. Therefore who would you turn to for validation in life? You can only turn inwards, to accept yourself and be the best you can be (with the resources you have) and know that you and your life are in perfect order.

In light of this - does the opinion of others have anything to do with you? And can you live with the possibility that your opinion is not valued by some of the people on earth? And can you live with the possibility that some people don't like you? And can you give yourself permission to not like everyone either?

SOUL TRIBE

One vital part of your contract as a human being is to work with and learn from others. You therefore need to create space for others to join in your life. If you are feeling lonely, making the effort to go out and find someone to befriend you might be daunting. Also when you meet others you might find that your 'needs' overwhelm them.

Building your soul tribe is heart centred work. It is calling out to your source energy and guides to support you in meeting up with people who will nurture and support you and others who will seek your nurture and guidance. Take action to follow your dreams: If your dream is to be a famous singer, and you are only singing in front of the mirror and recording on your phone, then go and find other people to sing with. A local choir, another band, a drama group. Find others that share your passions, maybe they are online, but one day you might meet. Seek out different people for different reasons. If your passions are more solitary, like writing then join a writing group, a reading group, even if they are online, you will be connecting with others and building your social circle.

Sharing your wisdom with others will help you grow too.

Letting Loose The Ego

Self esteem is a vital part of living in a community. Knowing yourself, being confident in who you are and being confident enough to assert your choices all add up to a powerful person within the community.

When this power is out of balance, then the community is at risk. Managing the ego is a skill, an art form and you have already started mastering it through the steps in this stage of the journey. You need to know your power and strength, and you may need to assert your knowledge in the face of a community at risk and use this strength to lead. You might not be the greatest orator, but your passion and calm confidence with humility will guide you to achieve your goals.

Negotiation

The art of negotiation rests in neutrality. When you are not triggered by others' opinions and attacks, even if this is personal and hurtful, you stand in power and strength.

Simple Steps

Make your request - clear and simple. Listen with wide open ears to the response, read unspoken words as clearly as the spoken and read between the lines to discover intention and any weakness. Check your own triggers, emotions and fears by breathing through them and stand firm in the intention you set.

Withdraw graciously with gratitude for the opportunity and express appreciation for the information they shared. However large or small the negotiation, you must be willing to hear alternative views with honesty and integrity, retaining authenticity and honour and seeking information in order that you can review and prepare a stronger case.

Gossip And Slander

Keeping your counsel is a sign of great spiritual maturity. When others enter into drama, gossip or slander, do not join in. Walk away if you can, knowing that if they are willing to do this to another they are willing to do this to you. If challenged, state firmly without accusation what you believe "if you have something to say, it should be said to the person, not discussed behind their backs".

If someone has harmed you, it is natural that you will want to validate your position and gain support. How you choose to do this and with whom is greatly important. Choose a mature person who will hold space for you to share your story, who will enable you to heal the hurt and find your path back to forgiveness and let go of the pain of the experience. Then it is important for your own preservation to take this experience to Mystery to unpack and extract all the learning you can.

Learning about yourself is a lifetime journey, it is in connection with others that you will learn the most. Whether you are a visual, auditory, or 'by experience' learner, there will always be another influencing that learning.

The most valuable people are those that will hold up a mirror for you. Mirrors have no image themselves, they are only a tool for reflection. When someone holds up a mirror for you, they might directly talk about your responses and reactions to events. They might point out that you are putting yourself down or limiting your life with your words and self effacing statements.

Mirrors can also show you unhealed parts of yourself by repetitive experiences in life. One of the greatest mirrors are found in intimate relationships, each one showing you your lack of self love. If you are addicted to dysfunctional relationships, they are just a mirror guiding you to your own truth. Take time out and learn how to love yourself.

Loving Yourself

As you connect more to the lovelight within, as you spend more time getting to know who you are, the reason you are here and how wonderful and gifted you are in soul energy, the more you will begin the journey of self love. Each time you challenge the feeling that you are unworthy, broken, unhealed, unlovable and seek a higher truth, you unveil the hard layers that life has coated you with. The more you put on the lens of love and care for your heart, your body, mind and spirit, the gentler and more loving you will feel about yourself. And the deeper and richer the journey of self love, the easier it will be to love others.

Shedding egoic nature and transforming it into self love, acceptance and forgiveness, enables you to more readily accept another despite their flaws and perceived imperfections. You begin to see the other in a new light, seeing frailty in their humanity and magnificence in their energetic form. You see behind the veil that they project, you begin to see light in their darkness and are able to reveal their beauty and guide them to self acceptance.

The physical form is in itself magical, it might be scarred by life, deformed by physical disease or accident. It is a mask, a shell, a vehicle of your love light in energetic form and the deeper you go on your journey of transformation, the more beauty you will see in others and they will in you. You will also see how the burdens of life have embittered some people and how they are so locked into the hard shell of protection that no lovelight can be seen. If they were a tree in this forest, they would stand alone, no creature would play in their branches, no fruit would grow and no beetles would forage between their roots and if you were able to see underground, you would not find any root attachment to other trees or mycelium growing near.

This tree is 'cut off' from community and life. In the process of being cut off, it bears disease and creates risk for the life around it, it will not be long before the life force dies in such isolation. The embittered person has succumbed to their fate, the hurt and damage they experienced was so deep that they have protected themselves with an impermeable layer to prevent any further despair. Should this person be in your life and be a person you love, then your role is to shine lovelight onto them with the intention that their layers of pain will soften and that they will begin to feel safe and secure enough to embark on their journey of transformation.

In a community, there is a wide array of personalities, cultures, beliefs and backgrounds, the very soil it inhabits absorbs the vibrational energy of the people. If it were a garden it might be bright and beautiful or a barren wasteland that has been used as a tip. Each community holds its own vibration and projects that to the world.

Vibrational Energy

Within the forest, you can see the trees, flowers and the fruit. You may be able to glimpse some of the wildlife here, but mostly they go about their business without notice. The higher your vibration, the more you will see. You are raising your vibrational energy as you read through this book and as you practise the steps, the weight of your past, thoughts and words are lifting and your vibrational energy rises with it. You will notice that you feel lighter, less burdened and more hopeful. As this energy lifts, there is more space to fill and you will begin to see more details in life, you will notice the petals on the flowers, the markings of the tree, in new ways and you might begin to notice that you are feeling more at 'one or peace' in nature.

There will be a skip in the step and feelings of joy and excitement will become more alive in you, desire for darker thoughts and stimuli might subside. You will notice your moods dipping and rising and this inner awareness will enable you to make healthier choices. You will feel more able to reach out to others, to notice when they are draining you of energy, and more able to notice the lessons they are teaching you.

Your judge's wig will be removed far quicker than before as you notice your words and thoughts about others and how these add layers of limitation to them and further prevent their liberation.

You may even find that you no longer need to sugar coat the difficulties of life as you explore healthier ways to live and respond to events around you. You will be making healthier choices about the people you spend time with, how to avoid toxic people and how to live an abundant life with the people you choose to spend time with.

Resilience

Consider the trees in the forest, how they stand despite the weather, the storms and the frosts, they may be laden with snow or fruits and yet, they stand. They are firmly planted in the ground and this enables their long trunks with wide branches to sway in the wind, to bend and not break and to restore themselves quickly.

If you compare yourself to a tree, how rooted are you? And what ground are you rooted into? In order to be a resilient human, you need to be grounded in truth: Your Own. To be confident in who you are, self assured yet flexible enough to consider alternate viewpoints and new concepts.

You will be seen as having wisdom beyond your years as you listen with open ears, alert and ready to respond and manage any triggers without reacting. This is skilled work that takes practice and persistence but the effort is worthwhile.

Being grounded in your daily routines and habits and on top of life with all its distractions, whilst enjoying the fruits of your labours enables you to be prepared. In practical terms, this means having your affairs in order, ensuring good financial management and a well stocked food supply. These might be unexpected suggestions in the process of unveiling the magic of you, however in the building of resilience, being prepared and ready for unexpected events is paramount.

Take time to organise your life and notice how that creates confidence and reassurance and have fun in your actions.

One of the keys to resilience is wearing the lens of love for yourself and others, not allowing yourself to fall into the trap of self effacing mantras or vitriolic thoughts about another.

Every Situation Is An Opportunity For Learning

Maintaining this philosophy will build your strength, determination and resilience and in so doing will release veils that have kept your true nature hidden. When challenges come and they will, remember that it's possible that the protagonist is one of your soul group and you might have contracted for this exchange. This thought creates curiosity and leads you towards reflection rather than blame.

Harmony

Creating harmonious communities requires each person to connect to others with kindness, forgiveness and compassion. As you have seen in the forest, there is a coming together to support and nurture, to bend with all of nature to ensure the collective are safe and preserved. In life, this is your role, to come together with others and build connections. Seeking to raise others up, to encourage, enable and guide. To look upon each person with love and have the wisdom to know when to step forward or stand back.

It doesn't mean subjugating yourself for those less fortunate than yourself, but it does mean to ensure their basic needs are met before your greater needs are fulfilled. Feed the hungry and clothe the poor whilst facilitating their independence and a sustainable future by directing them to opportunities for growth.

And if you are the one who is in need, retain your humility in the face of difficulty and accepting loving support when offered. There are many ways to serve each other and to create harmony in your own life and those who share your community.

Kindness is generated from love, a heart full of love can only wish others well. When you are looking through the lens of love, life is softer, the harsh edges fade and you are able to see more clearly. You can see the unhealed aspects of a person and in this realisation can be more considerate of their position, seeking only to support their healing and transformation. You look upon them without bias, prejudice or preconception seeing only their light that is hidden and appealing to their strengths and capacities to support their growth.

When others are unkind to you, without thought or reason, do not take this personally, they are only showing you their unhealed parts and giving you an opportunity for growth. Take their words or actions to mystery and explore any aspect of you that is in need of attention.

Treat yourself with great kindness when you discover your own unhealed parts, lean into others that love you and draw on their strength. Develop more ways to understand yourself, and give yourself permission to be a learner on this road of life in the knowledge that you learn by your mistakes.

Notice your language and find gentle ways to deliver your thoughts and opinions. As you build a kinder language towards yourself you will find that you are kinder to others and can negotiate relationships fraught with complexity with a greater ease.

LOVE

When you love, you love with all your heart and soul, you love with every cell of your being, love has no beginning or end, love Is. You are love, you are the embodiment of love which is not an emotion or a mental process.

Emotion Of Love

The emotion of 'love' is a veil through which you are beguiled into believing that you are separated from it and need to find it and feel adrift without it. Whether or not another 'loves you' is irrelevant, the feelings that are generated when someone withdraws love from you is fear. Fear is the absence of love. You are never absent from love, and without the generated belief that love is an emotion then you would not know fear.

When you completely understand this then you will know the greatest peace, you will embody love and be a beacon of light for others. In your journey of unveiling the magic of you, this is probably the most profound change. You will now need to learn how to navigate this new understanding, first take time to consider any generated feelings, explore all reactions and responses with kindness and justice. Write in your journal about love, considering all of your understanding until this revelation and how you have experienced lack of love, heartbreak and fear.

Simple Steps   ⓟ3:2

Take yourself into mystery and wrap yourself completely in

radiant golden light. Make a powerful connection with the golden thread and in your imagination rise above yourself, high up into the sky, into the cosmos, above the stars and look down upon yourself, shining bright. Notice the other bright lights around you and how the earth is littered with lights, even the oceans brimming with the light of all life on the planet, the trees and plant life are alive with lovelight.

Notice that there is no separation, each light connected to the other, a whole mass of lights operating as one in harmony. The air surrounding the planet is filled with light, earth itself is love and as you rise higher you see other planets and notice that they too are alight with love, the whole cosmos, the whole of creation is love. Nothing separates it, as even the space between is filled with lovelight.

Find yourself drifting towards a bright light and coming to rest near it, it is lovelight energy, you feel drawn to it and get closer, it speaks to you and welcomes you, inviting you to enter into the energy of Love. There is a seat and you rest there, drinking in this powerful pure energy of love, every cell in your body feels alive and whole and it is as if your mind and your emotions are being reorganised as you sit here beginning to fully understand the power of love. You are being transformed as layer upon layer of separation, loneliness and unfulfilled desire drop away, you see that you are and always were loved, because you are love. Each time you felt loved was when the other activated the love inside you and each time you felt loving was when you were activating the others self love.

As the veil is lifted and the layers fall away, you realise how much love was shown to you throughout your life, by strangers, teachers, family, friends, animals, plants and trees, and how when you rejected their love it was because you had forgotten for that moment who you are. Stay here, wrapped in the light of love until you are ready, empowered and with greater understanding to return to life complete in the knowledge that you are love.

You will want to take time to assimilate this understanding, to experiment with it in your mind, in your writing and in your relationships. It is not 'common knowledge' it is not necessarily something that everyone will understand, so find your path, find ways to test this out, to put your hand on your heart and feel that energy of love coming to you from others and when you send love out to others imagine that the golden thread links you all together.

The more information you process, the more awake and alive you are beginning to feel, others will begin to notice, they will sense that you are holding yourself differently and that you are reacting and responding to life circumstances with a different energy. This might cause some separation, a belief that in some way you are superior to them, that you have become highfalutin and have stopped speaking their language. How do you manage this?

You can only manage others' opinions of you by managing yourself. Taking your thoughts and feelings to mystery, asking for guidance and support and maintaining your balance. There is a human need to belong, to be a part of something and to feel accepted and loved. People conform in groups to that end by changing their image, their thoughts and their behaviours to match. As you are on a new journey, you will feel out of alignment with some of these images, thoughts and behaviours. Only you can know whether you are prepared to make those changes, which might mean that you choose to withdraw from that group.

If the group is a work colleague situation, where you cannot leave, then you must find ways to be comfortable in your own skin, to stand firm in your own power and maintain your balance. In time your colleagues will be drawn to you, they will individually seek your energy and light, be patient, send out love to all and relax into your new way of being.

If the group are your family members, lean into them, ensure they know you love them and send them love every day, do your best not to engage in conflict and find ways to become self contained if family dynamics are difficult. Be kind, helpful and infuse the home with love. Take yourself into mystery to resolve any hurt or discomfort and shine your light of love into the family home.

Forgiveness

Holding on to past hurts, words spoken, physical harm, impacts each cell of your body, it is like a sheath that covers your energy. It can harden your heart which causes resistance to life and all that it offers. The pain endured becomes a story and the story once told will grow and grow with each telling. You might begin to define yourself and your relationships by this story and in so doing become toxic. Do you remember the tree in the forest that had become diseased and isolated? All too often when holding on to these stories, they attract more of the same and you might find that life is out of flow as you are less and less in alignment with All that Is which is Love.

In the forest all life works in harmony, when another is hurt, the whole forest comes together to heal, to bring their energy to the hurt one and offer support through the process. The hurt one draws on this energy to heal, it accepts what happened and aligns with the healing process to ensure that it can use its strength wisely. How much energy does it take to hold on to past hurts? More than it takes to love yourself back to health.

Simple Steps

Accept what has happened, it is a fact. Sit with your feelings, write them down, cry them out. Talk about it with a wise and trusted person who is someone who will not get caught up in the drama. Look at the path before you, the possible futures: See what potential impact holding on to the hurt will have.

Ask yourself some serious questions: Will holding on to this benefit my future? Am I willing to let this go for the sake of my future? Will letting go mean forgetting? Will letting go mean my freedom? Take your situation to mystery and ask for support from your guides.

The process of forgiveness is many layered, by taking these steps, you will learn ways to forgive that suit your personality, you will see how the act of forgiveness sets you free to live your life and it may indeed impact on those that hurt you, but at this time that is not your concern. The person or people who hurt you are making their life choices, and you are making yours. They hurt you once: and in the process of forgiveness that stays at once. The alternative: each time you tell that story they are hurting you again and again. Remember you are Love, every cell of your being is Love, take off the sheath that hides you from that truth, the veil that has held you in a belief that love can be won and lost and set yourself free to be the powerful light to light up our world.

Relationships

We have focussed on relationships between life in the forest and your relationships in the world, let us now talk about your relationship with All that Is and your guides.

Can you imagine a family of souls that radiate love, laughter, joy and peace, who live their lives with the sole purpose of serving each other, learning, creating and supporting others. Can you imagine this space, where harmony is natural, when 'what if' scenarios are generated for the pure joy of creation? Where everyone remembers who they are and are content and at peace with that?

On the journey of awakening to who you really are, you can use your imagination to spend time in your soul family. Getting to understand the very essence of life in All that Is, learning to operate from a powerful place of cooperation and harmony. Also to build a relationship with your own soul energy in order that you can know the very heart of you and gain further clarity around your mission here on earth.

The Journey To All That Is

Take yourself into mystery, connect deeply to the radiant golden light and the golden thread, filling each cell and your aura space until you are completely at peace. Reach out your hand to take hold of the golden thread and in your imagination, see yourself floating along through all time and space holding the thread until you reach its source.

On arrival wait to be greeted and embrace your guide for this journey. Follow them through the corridors of your imagination, observing all that is happening around you. When you enter into the great space where your soul family are, you will notice the light has changed as you let loose your body to become as one with your family. They are in their Energy Bodies and you can recognise them and see elements of your earthly friends and family. They are busy creating together, laughing, playing, teasing and having fun. They invite you to join in and bring your creative gifts to their discussions.

You are drawn to one energy body, you can feel a deep and special connection and move towards them. The energy body greets you and invites you to move to a quiet place, you sit and talk about your current life and discuss your progress and the bonds of connection become greater as you spend time together, merging your thoughts and words. They tell you stories of your many lives and help to unpack some of your questions. This is your soul connection, the one you have been calling on every day of this journey and you are filled with the power of love.

Then it is time to leave and your guide collects you and takes you on a magical tour of All that Is. You see the great halls with many soul families, the schools, the fields of flowers, fruits and trees, the animals, birds, fish, insects and flying creatures, some that you recognise and many that you don't. And then you find yourself back at the start of the Golden Thread where you embrace your guide and begin your journey home.

You arrive back where you started and sit for a while

considering all you have learned and how this knowledge will impact your life. You know deep inside your heart that you will never feel lonely again and know that you have all you need right now to create the future you desire with a deep sense of who you really are. Rest in these thoughts and return to All that Is whenever you need.

When People Let You Down

There will be times in your life when you find yourself disappointed with another, do not take this personally, sit with those feelings and explore the root of your pain. This review might bring up some deeply held beliefs that were generated by others' stories or your own experience. The lens you are viewing this through is fear, the lens of fear fools you into feeling separate and alone, and this is where you can generate a new paradigm to live by.

When you review situations without emotional attachment you set yourself free of all of the angst there is in the world. Without emotion, you are free to experience life with curiosity, valuing all experiences with equal measure and determining whether you want to experience this again. For example, you enjoy a certain activity, this activity requires another to participate with the same degree of passion as yourself. Will you look around your friendship group and encourage one of them to be as passionate about this activity as you? Or will you seek out new contacts that are already passionate about that activity?

You are looking forward to an event, you have everything ready to attend and your friend lets you down at the last minute. Is there any hesitation in you to attend on your own, or do you decide not to go and feel disappointed. This is your life, and like the tree in the forest, it is your choice, to decide how much you will enjoy life. The tree is an individual, it is dependent on the forest for abundance of life, but it is not codependent. It can survive alone and thrive.

When there are unrealistic expectations, the opportunity for disappointment is rife. In the event of a break in a relationship, when another leaves or denies you a return of feelings, this is an opportunity to review your life and expectations. Can you trust that this is right for you and your future, can you allow the other freedom to leave with your blessing, can you accept that the other doesn't return your feelings?

When you find that place where you know love is, that you are love and that nothing separates you from that, you will seek different relationships with others. The personal power you hold will be attractive to others and you will be attracted to people with the same vibrational qualities that you generate yourself.

In intimate relationships you will seek only to support the other on their journey. If that journey leads them away from you, you will encourage them along their path of transformation, knowing that one day - maybe in a different lifetime your paths will meet again. As the trees support each other through their underground network of roots, so too can you 'underpin' the lives of people you connect with.

When you walk through the forest of life, you will meet many people, some like the birds who migrate, will come to rest in your life for a time and others will raise their families around you. Celebrate each opportunity of life, the expression of love and seek only to shine your lovelight on others, knowing that will attract love back to your life.

You have learned here that you are deeply and inextricably connected with All that Is, within the metaphor of the forest, you can see that each part of life works harmoniously with the other. This is equally true for humans on this planet. You are here for the shortest time, when measured against the millenia and civilisations gone before on planet Earth. Making the very best use of your time here, is an honour and a privilege and one not to be wasted or frittered away with meaningless chatter, negative self talk or feelings of isolation and loneliness.

Every story you have told throughout your life has led you to this moment . Without these stories you would be in a different place and time and not be in relationship with those you are and if you were a tree, you would not be planted in this forest. Therefore every story whatever it held brought you to this moment of now, which leads to the question - do you like what you have now? Is this where you are meant to be? Does this story have potential to lead you towards your dream? Will this story help you succeed in life and achieve your goals? And IF by chance you know that you are in the wrong place, then what can you do to change this?

Simple Steps   Ⓟ3:4

Go into mystery, call in your guides, imagine a circle of bright white light all around you. There are other energy balls of light surrounding and you are not alone and the vibrational energy in this space is light and bubbly. You feel like a bubble in a large bottle of fizzy water, bouncing and moving along with all of these other energy balls. You are in a tube moving forwards, scooting downwards, twists and turns at high speed. All the energy balls are laughing with you, this is fun.

Your journey ends in a cut crystal glass and you look around at all of the energy balls in this beautiful space, the light is reflecting and rainbows are scattered all around. You followed where life was leading you, leading to your purpose and look how beautiful it is, full of promise and service.

As you reflect upon your journey, you can only see the light, the laughter and the fun. Yet you recall your concerns and anxieties about getting it right and wonder where they are now as you float happily. Your image rewinds and you find yourself going backwards up through the tube and into your now and the very first question you asked of your guides.

They tell you... You can decide what you want to do, you have free will, you can choose to go this way or that way. You will make mistakes, take wrong paths and find yourself exactly where you are. All the better for the learning as whichever path you take, leads home, it leads to where you came from.

Both the hard or the easy path will bring untold riches to your life so: Make choices that make your heart sing.

Make choices for your own sense of self. Make choices to serve others. With love as your guiding force, you cannot go wrong.

Remain in this place until you have found your peace again. Bring yourself back out of mystery and take time to assimilate all you have learned. Write, journal, create vision boards, talk to friends and family and your guides. Ask yourself where you are on your journey now and whether the steps you have taken supported your response to Isis' intention:

> *I am wanting to show people how to live harmoniously with others - to challenge them to step back from their thoughts and a need to be right - I want them to know that they are a small cog in the wheel of life and their role is vital and they do not need to vie for superiority.*

CLIMBING
THE HIGHEST
MOUNTAIN

T his stage is like a butterfly breaking out of its cocoon, a chick breaking out of its shell, this is an awakening to the magnificence of life without fear, life without greed and life without controls. The biggest limitation for all humans is the mind, the thoughts that are generated there, the words formed and the beliefs that follow. When you challenge your own thinking, it is different from when you challenge another's, but remember the majority of your thoughts and beliefs are entrained.

INTRODUCTION

There is comfort in the sound of your own voice, and security in your beliefs, change is inevitable but there is resistance. The 'what if' questions return as you begin to make changes in your attitude, beliefs and your lifestyle. People are starting to notice and there might be feelings of being alien to those with whom you were once greatly connected. Letting go of your former identity is a challenge and this is where you begin.

There is nothing to fear. When you are in mystery, fast forward to a time in the not too distant future, to see how these changes have raised your vibration and elevated your thinking to a place of confidence and accord with the highest vibration of love. Go at your own pace, this is a lifelong journey, the more you bump into life, the more you will discover the benefits of your transformation and learning.

The Climb

When you stand at the bottom of a very high mountain the climb looks impossible, it is hard to see where the tracks lead. The task seems monumental and you begin to challenge yourself. Fear might creep into your mind, what if questions build pictures in your mind that feel insurmountable, doubt fills you and you risk giving up before you begin.

Today you stand at the bottom of a mountain, we will call it "The Mountain of Transformation" and I'd like you just to step back, turn around and look for a place where you can sit and observe, where silently you can ponder the possibilities of climbing this mountain of transformation.

Find yourself a space, a quiet space where you can sit and look, plan and prepare what you will need for the journey. The first thing you need for any transformation is a reason, purpose and vision. Create an hour where you will be undisturbed. Create a space that is comfortable and pleasing to you. You will need a timer, pens and paper and a glass of water.

STEP 1:
In this place I'd like you to find your breath, just observe it quietly and gently and when you feel calm open your eyes: Set a timer 10 minutes and without thinking, allow your intuition the freedom to write 20 intentions for this next step on your spiritual journey to climb the Mountain of Transformation. Stop when the timer rings even if you haven't created 20 intentions. If this is a struggle, just play with ideas.

STEP 2
Close your eyes, Take a breath and then review the 20 intentions to see which one stands out, we will call this your Primary Intention. It may change through this process and that is OK but for now this is where you can start.

STEP 3
With a new sheet of paper and a pencil, write down your primary intention as a header, take a moment to think about this and start writing, adding more detail along the way, remembering if you can't think - just make it up, take your time, there is no rush. The transformation that you desire is dependent on clarity around this primary intention. When you have finished writing, breathe into that intention by reading it out loud as many times as you need to to 'feel it' in your body, 'understand it' with your mind and 'see it' through your eyes.

STEP 4
Go into mystery: We are going to go on another journey of

the imagination: Imagine somewhere in the distance you can see yourself at the top of the mountain of transformation. Notice what you notice, all the fine details of the expression on your face, your body language, the light energy in your aura space. Imagine that you can fly over and step into the image. Feel what it feels like, what do you notice about yourself? What are you noticing about having completed this task?

Look back towards your now, notice your learning, your struggles, who was with you, who is championing you, notice the naysayers, the people that discouraged you, notice what challenges were personal to you and what memories came up and what story evolved out of this. In your imagination: walk back along the path to now and step back fully into your own body. Take a breath and bring to mind all the key points you have discovered here.

STEP 5

Write key points that you wish to remember. Create an understanding from this exercise to really hone down the steps you will need to take before you attempt this journey.

Repeat this exercise with some or all of the intentions you wrote in the 20 intentions exercise as you move forward in your journey. When you are on the journey of transformation you don't have to take everything apart but you do need to dig into your psyche and deep into your culture and belief systems.

Unlike the acorn, who knew the Oak tree that lay at the heart of it, you have been entrained or programmed throughout your life. What you have been shown and told has become the truth. This might have come through family, community, education, politics and religion. Any belief you brought with you on this journey of life has been lost and much of what you have been told is limiting, even that which is in service to all.

Alongside this, you might have stories from your own experience that are binding you. The impact of these stories can make profound changes to your belief system and have caused you to fear. This fear may cause you to act or respond in certain ways which prevent you moving forward in the direction of your dreams. When you came to earth you did not know fear, you had complete trust and a very clear plan.

Unwrapping these stores is where you begin to climb the mountain of transformation and there is wisdom in beginning this journey with easier, less painful issues. Otherwise it would feel like the challenge of climbing Mount Everest which would seem insurmountable from most people's position today.

In order to climb this mountain, you need to be as strong and healthy in mind and body as you are able. You need supporters, people who will champion and train you, you will need to make a commitment to work for your own growth, peace and transformation.

I cannot paint a picture of ease as any real transformation will dig deep and modify many aspects of your life. When I moved from obscurity, it was not with ease, you know many stories that were told and believed and are still spoken of today. Making changes can be challenging to people around you and we will explore methods to manage this through these pages.

Leaning in to your guides on a daily basis when you enter into mystery. Using discernment to approach each 'story' that needs unravelling and being patient with yourself as you take tentative steps towards your future. The journey might be rocky at times and if you find that it unbalances you, then stop, pull back and breathe into all the changes you have made. Allow the learning to assimilate, keep filling yourself with Radiant Golden Light and nurturing your needs. This journey is life long - here you are learning the 'how to' and you can return here anytime you need.

If you were climbing an actual mountain, you might hire a sherpa, certainly for Mt Everest. In life, draw close to those who are already on this journey, those with wisdom to support you and build a tribe of like minded people across the world who understand what you are doing and why.

Also build ever stronger connections with your

Highest Wisdom, all your spiritual guides, angels, your soul tribe and those who are in spirit who can guide you. You do this through your daily practice of bringing in the light to cleanse and heal and bringing your intention into the space for inspiration and instruction. Read books, watch videos, attend training, remain curious at all times and take all the learning to mystery to sift out only what is right for your journey.

The stories that you will be unravelling have come from many sources, you may well be carrying the stories of your ancestors and some stories might have skipped a generation. If you experience unusual fears and anxieties that don't feel like they belong to you, this might be the root.

Generational Stories

As you learned in the Hall of Records and the Library, every word spoken or thought is imprinted in the collective, this means that we are all subject to picking up the energy of old stories. Buildings, towns, cities will hold the stories of all those who lived or passed through. When you move into a new house, town or country, you will be picking up the vibrations of all those who have gone before, think of it as being in the DNA of that space.

As you move around different locations you will notice that energetic frequencies differ, this is because the atmosphere of the whole area is completely imprinted with the story. When you find a place where you feel comfortable, it has an energetic frequency that aligns with yours. Conversely when you are uncomfortable, you are out of alignment with the energies there.

Becoming aware of the imprinted stories in your life will support transformation and like all the stories that you have worked on so far you can bring these back to mind and work on them using the same tools. It is important to find the root of any story that is impinging on your life today. These roots, like tree roots that we spoke about in Wandering through the Forest, tell you that the connections between you and your ancestors remain very strong through the connections that were made throughout timelines.

In All that Is, these stories are shared and all the learning is extracted. It may be that part of your purpose and your mission is to resolve these ancestral or generational stories. Your guides will be able to find these generational stories through the records that they hold and will be able to support you in your mission to resolve them.

Can you think of a story that is rife in your family history, it might be a sickness, wealth, poverty, a love of gardening. Choose one that you feel might be impinging on your forward movement, one that feels out of alignment with the essence of you.

Simple Steps   Ⓟ4:1

Take yourself into Mystery

Bring in the golden light through the golden thread and Pull through the radiant golden light. See yourself with the energies flowing around you and encasing you. Bring to your guides the intention of finding the root of e.g. 'poverty thinking' that is in your family history.

Ask them to guide you to the very first event where this idea was created. Imagine that you are drifting from your seat and rising up over your whole lifetime and further into the mist of time

Imagine that you are flying all the way through to the place where this event occurred. Imagine that you can see the people, the landscape, the architecture, the clothes. Listen in to the event, to understand the dynamics, the expressions and the conversations that are occuring

When you have a great understanding, drift down into the event and speak with the people. Share your wisdom and knowledge of the future and guide them. When you feel that you have made the necessary impact

Drift out of the image and rise higher until the image fades. Fly back over all of the lifetimes, the years and as you pass all of the events where poverty thinking was present, send your love and healing to them and keep moving forward until you return to your now.

Hover over your present state and send love and clearing down to your own situation. Drift back down and when you believe that your 'being' has assimilated all of the changes drift back into your physical being.

Check that the cords are all broken and if you feel they aren't: Imagine a cord that represents the root of the problem in your hand and hand it out into the universe, asking your wise guides to complete the task and watch as the cord evaporates into thin air.

Take some gentle breaths and return to your now. Allow the experience to assimilate and sit with these new thoughts. Write in your journal how it feels to be free of that concept. I chose poverty thinking, because it encompasses everything: money, health, love and spirit. And is often the cause of this is Fear.

Money

Money is only an exchange, it has been corrupted by greed and is a force that causes much pain. How do you move from poverty to abundance?

You have severed the generational cord which will allow you to move forward, to make the changes you desire. Having lived with this story for so long it will naturally take time to assimilate and to move from a poverty mindset to abundance.

Let's call this 'base camp' a place where you will find one of your greatest powers in knowing that you have wealth beyond measure and abundance flows towards you.

Simple Steps   Ⓟ4:2

Go into Mystery: Imagine that you are in a room that is lined with gold, pure gold, everything is gold, the seat you are sitting on, the cup that you are drinking from, this is the palace of abundance. There is sweet music drifting through an open window and you find that you are drifting deeper and deeper into mystery.

The golden seat morphs with your body as it relaxes and comes to rest. You are in 'heaven', you know this because you can see your angels, your guides and your loved ones smiling down at you. You feel good, content, free of any concerns but most of all you feel loved, how good does this feel?

You wake slightly from your slumber and see before you a table of fruits of all shapes and sizes, a banquet of love. Around the table sit all your loved ones with chatter and laughter ringing aloud. Looking around you recognise this familiar room. You look down at your seat and see that it is your favourite armchair. As you look around at the faces that you love, you are in a state of bliss. Putting your hand upon your heart, you feel the love of all those who have lived and will live and you know your wealth. The golden room falls away and you are sitting there complete, understanding that you are already abundant in love and possession.

Now spend time with your guides, discussing your wealth, fears and needs and when you are ready. Return, through your breath, to the room. Write in your journal and allow all feelings to flow, bring into the light your financial situation and honestly appraise your income and outgoings. Do what you can to balance your finances and find your peace.

Notice the language you use around money, wealth and abundance and do what you can to change your mind, attitude, words and approach to your own financial circumstance.

Health

Health is your priority, take responsibility for your body's functioning both inside and out. Your body, mind and spirit are all interconnected, when one aspect of you is out of order, it impacts the whole. Throughout your transformation you will find that as you begin to love and value yourself more, you will start to notice what is happening in your body and understand how the symptoms you experience are warning signs of a dysfunction at a deeper level of your being.

Bringing yourself into the radiant golden light of love every day will speed your healing and also your intuitive understanding of these symptoms. Bring your needs to your guides and All that Is, asking for support to make the changes needed for a healthy life.

Love

The glue that holds you together, that links body, mind and spirit is love. It is impossible to live fully, wholly, completely without love. Where do you find the magic of love within you? Every cell, every breath you take, every heartbeat, is pumping love around you. The air you breathe, the fresh vegetables you eat are filled with love, love is living breathing throughout the planet, you are drenched in love at all times.

The opposite of love is fear, when you engage in fear, you reduce your power, your strength and your capacity to live a full rich life. Your body weakens, your mind weakens and your connection to All that Is is reduced. Dragging yourself out of fear is harder the longer you have resided there. This is the highest mountain.

How do you manage the yin and yang of life, the ability to find neutral, where you can manage those darker thoughts and experiences without plummeting into fear and turning off the tap of love? You maintain your daily practice, you make commitments to yourself about your day to day living and the lens through which you choose to experience life and love.

How does this work day to day? This works by making a choice every day to be the best you can be. A choice to believe that Everything is in Perfect Order. A decision to accept people are already doing their best with the resources that they have. A commitment to hold yourself in power, knowing that you are far more than a physical being. A commitment to be honest with yourself. Maintaining an understanding that everything that happens has a deeper, more valuable meaning and a commitment to finding it.

A daily expression of gratitude, for your body, mind and spirit, those you share your life with, your possessions, your teachers, the facilities you have and the dreams that keep you buoyant. And finally and most importantly to LOVE. To fill yourself with earth and universal energy. To spread that energy out to the world. To share that energy with all the people & beings you meet. To be active in your listening. To be gentle in your thoughts. To be kind with your words.

MANAGING DIFFICULT PEOPLE

People wear their hurt on their faces and in their bodies. As you develop your skills you will be able to recognise fear, pain and despondency in people, just by their body language, their eyes, skin and hair. You will become attuned to those that lack a daily infusion of love.

When you meet these people, they might choose to project their pain, hurt, anger and hatred onto you. It is too much for them to bear on their own and are desperately seeking freedom from the prison they have built around them. They bump up against people because they need to steal energy to survive. Love is life force energy and they will feed on yours because they have cut off access to their own. This is why you feel drained and exhausted after spending time with them.

Because they are full of vitriol, bitter cruel words come out of their mouths. The lens they are choosing to view the world from is dark and hateful. In the cold light of day, would you take anything they say personally, would you consider their words to be wise and worth listening to? Would you heed their words?

Putting people in this context, enables you to understand why you have carried so many negative thoughts about yourself, especially if you were raised, educated or led by such a person. You might have encountered bosses that held this energy and felt contaminated by it.

If you lived with such a person, then the contamination will be deeper as they will have undermined your sense of self, created doubt and prevented you living at your highest potential

The time has come for you to shed these words, these beliefs and really to open up every cell to the receiving of healing energy, the light of love to rain down upon you and fill every aspect of your being.

Simple Steps   ℗4:3

Fill yourself with the radiant light of love every morning and throughout your day. See yourself as a shining light that all can see. Every time a thought, a memory or a pain reveals itself: Wrap it in a ball of light. Release it to the universe for transformation.

Create a ball of light in your hands. Mould the light into a golf ball size. Hold the light ball on your body where you feel the pain of those words or memories. Push the light in and watch it swirling away all memory, pain or dysfunction there. Watch the ball of light leave your body and rise high into the universe for transformation. Then fill yourself with love again.

Note: if the energy is stuck and you cannot move it in this simple way. Use one of the steps you have learned already that most suits your personality to examine, release and forgive.

Actions Speak Louder Than Words

The way you present to the world, is the way you will be perceived by the world. As an unknown Goddess, I dressed in the people's clothes to walk among them and heal them. Had I walked in with my light shining and wrapped in gold and silk, the people would not have accepted my help. They saw Gods as inaccessible and separate, they had much fear of us and were in many ways our servants. Walking amongst them required not only that I dressed differently, but also that I spoke their language and maintained simplicity in my being.

I do not suggest you make dramatic changes like this unless you are called to work in places that would require it. I also do not suggest that in order to work with the sick you become sick. When you completed the first meditation where you saw a desired image of yourself in the future, what did you notice, how did you feel looking at yourself? What changes did you make? When you stood in your body how different was that?

As you are dressing in the morning, take some time to look at yourself and critically appraise the projected image without judgement. Are you happy with it or do you want to make some changes?

What language does your projected image speak to people? Is it powerful, careless, casual, authoritative, easy, homely, fashionable, unique, outdated, avant garde? Does this describe you? And is this the description that will lead you forward to your dreams?

As you ponder on the language of your projected image, you might consider the language of your body, the way you hold yourself, ability to offer eye contact, how you express with your face, a slight tilt of the head to listen. Often unhappy people hide themselves in clothes but also in their body, crumpling up their spine with shoulders forwards, shuffling their feet as they walk and hiding their face behind hair or hoodie.

The more you develop a keenness about your own projected image and how you change it for different circumstances, the more you will be able to read other people's body language and pick up cues about their state of mind.

This section is about discernment, but like all the learning here, you start with yourself. The majority of your limitations are your own limitations, the ones you put on yourself and change can be as simple as polishing your shoes and ironing a crumpled shirt/dress. The mountains you climb do not have to be difficult, they often will disappear in a flash with the smallest of changes.

So build yourself up, climb those mountains with power, with love as your banner and conquer your limitations so that you can conquer the world.

Comparison & Competition

The cells in your body do not compete with each other, the brain and heart cells don't argue with each other about which one is the most valuable. They understand that they are both of equal importance. Each individual is a representation of the whole, each cell is vital for the whole organism to grow and develop the organism of humanity.

When there is damage to a series of cells in your physical body the whole organism is impacted and will produce chemicals to support healing. When there is damage in humanity, all humans are called to send out the light of love to support restoration of balance and order.

How does damage occur within the organism of humanity? Predominantly through physical changes in the core of the earth creating catastrophe, also carelessness with fire, intentional harm of the planet, virus, human frailty, competition, striving for power, dominance and fear. Much of this is played out in small ways in the playground and in larger ways in war. The root of which is fear and presented as comparison and competition.

Each culture brings with it a bench mark of beauty, of intelligence, strength and capacity. Making a decision about what is right or wrong, good or bad, acceptable or unacceptable behaviour. Those who seek to dominate, to be the God of the community will make rules and expect strict compliance, yet many of these rules are not made for the collective good, they are made for dominance, fear inducement and control.

A desire to be the best, get the best scores, achieve the highest position, to be respected, valued and adored are of a high vibration, purposeful, creative and will elevate the vibration of earth for all.

These desires coupled with aggressive competition, infer the person wants to be the best and most adored exclusively and in so doing are willing to disable others opportunities to achieve their intention. This is a lower or denser vibration.

The vibration of fear presented as aggressive competition is seen being played out in sports and business and is often hailed as good. It is good to strive to be the best but once it is at the expense of another, then conflict arises and unhealthy relationships might follow.

Those who are highly competitive and spend hours comparing themselves or their possessions with others, will find deep dissatisfaction in their lives. You have met these people, who seem to have it all, yet beneath the surface they are as pained as yourself. If this competition is coming from a third party, demanding excellence and determining your path, you might find yourself in conflict.

This brings us to another element of comparison and competition and that is expectation.

Expectation

The expectations you put upon yourself or that others create for you, might be the very reason you are limited in reaching your desires.

In an intimate or familial relationship there are certain expectations that each person agrees to, to ensure harmony and balance in the shared space. These are practical solutions to a shared vision. However when expectations relate to behaviours, beliefs and practices, then these must be discussed and agreed.

As a Goddess I was expected to behave in certain ways, but that was not an expectation of myself. I did what I had to do to comply, but I created far greater expectations upon myself, for the work my heart was calling me to. And here I am, still doing that work, in a completely different time and space.

The expectations of your heart: that deep and wonderful knowing and determination to fulfil your purpose comes from the very source of who you are. The mystery that you are beginning to understand more every day, the guidance, the direction of your spirit and the sensations you feel in your body when you enter into any thoughts, dreams or discussions about it.

When these expectations are driven by that innate knowing, the intuitive guidance and the pulse radiating through your whole body, then you know that you are on the right path. There is an excitement within you, a desire that is overflowing and you are single minded and focussed on achieving that goal.

When you look at your purpose, do you see any competition or comparison in it? Do you see that it is in service to the collective, that those who need this gift will find it, that you can embody your purpose and share it? Then you know you have reached that wonderful place of love.

Love is the source of all, it is in every cell of your body, it radiates through from earth, it is in your breath, it is real, tangible and complete. There is no comparison or competition in the heart of love. There is only service, first to yourself in self care, then to your intimate relationships, your community, your landmass and then the world.

You will also harness a strong desire for others to succeed, to be the best, get the best scores, achieve the highest position, to be respected, valued and adored, to be purposeful and creative, knowing that they will elevate the vibration of Earth for the benefit of all.

Your purpose may have many aspects to it, when you have fulfilled one, you will move onto the next. It is important that you keep dreaming and allowing flow with your purpose, being alert to new opportunities, directions and your dreams.

Simple Steps

If you are highly creative:
Create a vision board: Either using cut outs from magazines or Digital copy of images online. Randomly select all the images that you love, things you enjoy doing, activities that

make your heart sing. Lay them all out on your board and glue them together to make a beautiful piece of art.Display the board and meditate on these images.

If you are a word person:
Start a writing practice every day where you sit quietly and start writing, use prompts that inspire you: 'when I was a child I loved to....'Keep writing for a set time and if you get stuck write out your prompt again until the words flow. At the end of the week, read through and pull out key words, key themes and meditate on them.

Raise a discussion with Intimate connections: Ask people how they see you, what special qualities do they admire in you and what can they imagine you being if you were completely without limits.

Go into mystery: Seek guidance and direction from Source energy, your guides, angels, beings or loved ones

Play with ideas: Join a club and learn new things, enrol in a course of interest, volunteer in your community or the world. Get active and meet new people, do something different, eat something different. Read new and interesting books. Watch old and new films or documentaries. Take your camera on a date and see what it sees.

Extending yourself in this way will help you to discover latent interests and hidden talents. Moving forward with your purpose through the power of love will attract those to you that will guide, support and benefit from your offering.

Greed

You have discovered that there are those that have and those that have not, this is the order of life at this time, it will not always be this way. On your journey you will wake up to the times where you have experienced great need for material possessions. You will begin to see that some of these possessions are a form of greed. If we explore the dynamics of greed, we find that the root of greed is lack of love. This new 'thing' will define me, it will make me look good, it will attract others, it will fulfil me.

It is as if this 'thing' will make up for the lack of love in your life. Rather like a child wanting a new toy and obsessing over it until a parent succumbs for a quiet life. The new toy is played with, but doesn't satisfy, it is discarded and the latest toy that their peers are playing with becomes the newest demand.

Let us break down what is happening here: The child wants to belong and when the child has this new toy, they feel that they will be able to belong in the group. By the time the child has acted out and won, it is too late, the group have got bored with that toy and have new ones. The child has not got the approval of their peers, is angry with their parents and feels unloved.

The key here is the child wants to belong. Belonging holds a power, a connection and this is interpreted as Love. When you look outside yourself for love, you will not be satisfied. Love is in every cell of your body, you are love. It is your birthright and it is never withdrawn from you. Each time you pull in the light of love, you are complete. Material possessions can not bring you happiness, joy, peace or love as these are gifts of the essence of who you are... the magic and mystery of you. Greed is not just about personal possessions or materialism, it is also about Power, the great need for recognition and control.

Simple Steps

What holds power over you? What drives you forward? What is your heart's desire? Dig deep into these questions, without judgement:

Set aside some time where you will be undisturbed. Take some full breaths and settle yourself. Write each question in turn and set a timer (no more than 10 minutes).

Allow yourself freedom to write without correction, just allow the words to flow and remember that this is for your eyes only. When the timer rings: Start with the second question, then the third.

At the end of the process: Write down how you feel about the exercise then read through your answers and extract any learning. Take this learning to mystery and ask your guides for support as you make sense of all that you have learned.

As you grow in personal power, you will find the need for trinkets and the need to control others will diminish, you will find a deeper contentment within yourself and be more interested in controlling your own life and living in heart centred and simple ways.

The more you learn about yourself, your magnificence and power, the more Freedom you will find in life. Do not judge yourself for former actions that occurred before your transformation, however if there are people who you wish to make reparation with, then bring those to mystery and act under guidance.

THE POWER OF THOUGHT

From the moment you were born you have had this power, this amazing ability to conjure up pictures or sounds in your mind and make sense of them through the power of thought. These thoughts are generated by curiosity and the need to create order in your life to understand and apply this knowledge to support your safety and wellbeing.

As an infant, you might have felt strange having movement when for nine months you were encased in a bath of warm water with limited ability to move or control any aspect of your body's function. You discovered very quickly that you could make noise, vocalise your needs and eventually get your needs met.

Your need for food, shelter, warmth, comfort and love and the speed of response to your sounding added more thoughts which included feelings. These feelings generated more thoughts, I feel held, hungry, ignored, loved, safe, understood, wanted.

You began to define your life through these thoughts and developed skills to get your needs met and generated more thoughts about your caregivers and those around you.

You met strangers who smiled, ignored, scowled, laughed, played with you. These people created more thoughts about safety and the world you lived in. You became more aware of your body and would stare for hours at your hands and feet.

You started to have thoughts about yourself and what this body could do. You began the process of movement propelled by your own thoughts to make space for yourself in this world. Desire to reach the toy, desire for food, desire for love and the speed in which your desires were reached determined your understanding of self and your place in the world.

You began to understand that you generated different responses through different actions. If you smile and giggle and make lots of sounds then you receive attention from people who smile and make sounds like yours. If you were unhappy and needed something and made lots of sounds then some people made a lot of noise and looked unhappy and other people picked you up, smiled and made soothing sounds.

All of these first impressions of life and thought are imprinted in you today. Your experience as a young infant is alive in you now.

You have perfected your understanding of life, learned how to get a certain response from different people and are living the life you have created through your mind. Are the thoughts you think congruent with the life you desire? Or are they playing tricks on you and limiting you in some way?

Simple Steps

Using writing prompts again: Ask yourself a question that is relevant to your situation. Examples: Why am I invisible? Why don't people listen to me? Why does my anger leak out? How is my anxiety causing me to fail?

Breathe into the feelings of your question
Set yourself a timer (no more than 5 minutes)
Write your question and allow your mind just to answer, without hesitation or judgement. Allow the words to flow

After you have finished: Breathe and settle yourself. Read through what you have written and extract the learning from it. Take the learning to mystery, ask for guidance. Find resolution through any of the steps you have learned here that work well for you.

Mental Picture

You have learned that thoughts can be generated through feelings and now we will explore how the images you carry with you will generate thoughts also.

Simple Steps

Remember this morning when you began to get dressed? What was the first thing you did? Do you remember your first driving lesson? The first time you ate spicy food? The first time you paddled in the sea?

Every day your eyes receive thousands of stimuli, how do you select the visions to hold in memory? Mental Pictures that you associate with feelings are retained, the mind has no concept of good or bad, the nervous system makes no distinction between anxiety and excitement and yet if Fear is generated it will provide you with hormones to manage the situation in whichever way you are entrained to do. It is a survival instinct and the decision you make to keep you out of harm.

Your images play out in your mind, like a movie on a screen that you saw in The Library. Until these images are processed they hold a power over you and generate thoughts and actions that may lead you down difficult paths.

If in a guided meditation you are asked to take yourself to a safe and beautiful place, this will generate memories of places you have been that encompass happy and safe feelings, if you enter into that memory, the movie will begin to play, the colours will be sharp, the sounds rich and movement smooth. You will immediately return to the feelings on that day and all the imprints it had on your life going forward.

In a challenging situation, you will revisit an equivalent experience from the past. The movie will run in high technicolour, the feelings overwhelmingly powerful and the new person before you will be superimposed onto the image of the protagonist in the first image. All new people who bear resemblance or character will be perceived in the same way. This will impact your relationships and limit your opportunities.

Without making judgement, lean into the knowledge that each scenario you remember is there for you to extract all the learning from it which will support you going forwards. There are ways to manage the more challenging situations.

Simple Steps   ℗4:4

Take yourself into Mystery. Breathing into your feelings, knowing you are safe and protected. Choose a memory that has charge in it but no trauma. Choose the image you want to process and start the movie on the screen, watch the movie from beginning to end. Play it backwards, Imagine that the screen is getting smaller each time you play the movie. Now play it again and in reverse. The colours are beginning to fade and the image is getting smaller. Play it again: The colour is almost gone, the screen is so small that you can barely see the movies. Play it again: The sounds are now distorted and the image is barely visible, just a shadow playing on the screen. Play it again and the screen is blank.

Now focus on your feelings, wrap yourself in a hug. Notice your thoughts, how do you feel now?

WORDS

The words you speak or write are powerful, even those that are just formed in your mind. Remembering their power might support you going forward to consider what you are saying to yourself and others. Every word ever spoken stays around you. How powerful are those words and what potential impact are they having on you today?

Throughout the day strive to be mindful of your language, your self talk and begin to notice the statements that start with 'I am....' Begin to unwrap that daily until you find the 'I am' that is true and helpful to you. Notice the 'I can't' as well, what can you not do and is that the truth? Also the 'that's difficult, impossible, a struggle' and all of those limiting statements. It may take a lifetime to conquer all of these limiting words and that is ok. The journey of transformation lasts a lifetime and as you are aware it is a daily choice about how you present to the world and react to situations around you.

When you look through life with the lens of love it changes your language, you start to find kinder ways to speak about yourself and others. You increase your emotional literacy as you begin to express your feelings, those emotions that are generated by the power of love within you. As you fill yourself with love light and radiant golden light and release the old stories, you will experience the warmth of love from others and this in turn will enable you to be more aware of the emotions that govern your day.

Through the eyes of love, even the darkest day is manageable, as the raw emotions are filtered through love, compassion and forgiveness. You will continue to experience the full range of emotions but the charge in them will be reduced and recovery time shortened.

Emotional Literacy

When you are in touch with your emotions you build a language to understand the many states that govern your life. There are no judgements about the whole range of emotions that you feel, each one has validity and you will rank them in terms of healthy or unhealthy according to the situation.

If we review some feeling words in alphabetical order without any 'weight or measure' attached: Go through the list and see if there is a feeling that you associate with the words and what that means to you, also check if there is a story attached that needs further work. If for example you feel 'frustrated' a lot of the time: where did that come from, what can you learn from this - what is this feeling giving you? What is it saying to you?

Take each word you identify with and use it as a prompt to explore more thoroughly through writing about it for 5 minutes. If there is work to do, for example you are curious, how is this serving you today and is there anything else you can be doing with it? Also can you recognise this 'feeling' in others? And if you were to label this a positive or negative then begin to unwrap why you believe this.

Afraid, Angry, ANnoyed, Anxious, Ashamed, Balanced, Bored, Brave, Calm, Cheerful, Confident, Connected, Creative, Curious, Desperate, Drained, Energetic, Excited, Frightened, Frustrated, Furious, Gloomy Grateful, Guilty, Happy, Helpless, Hopeful, Hopeless, Humiliated, Hurt, Insecure, Inspired, Interested, Irate, Irritated, Joyful, Judged, Kindred, Lost, Loved, Loving, Mad, Miserable, Moody, Needy, Needed, Offended, Oppressed, Optimistic, Overwhelmed, Powerful, Powerless, Queasy, Radiant, Reflective, Rejected, Relaxed, Safe, Secure, Scared, Shocked, Stressed, Strong, Stunned, Superior, Surprised, Teased, Terrified, Tired, Trusted, Trusting, Uneasy, Unloved, Valued, Worried.

Each feeling is a valid expression. When you have started this work alongside all the other steps you are taking, you might find that you can build a healthy relationship with most of these descriptive words.

Are these feelings 'barometers' that you can use to recognise triggers and charge in your life and a warning sign that you are becoming out of balance and need to step back and heal?

Making relationships with all aspects of being human without judgement will allow you to leap forward in life, relationships, business and your spiritual transformation.

The process of transformation, like the butterfly emerging from its chrysalis, requires patience and persistence. If the process is interrupted or interfered with it can damage the butterflies abilities to live a full and fruitful life.

One might consider that humans have had their process of transformation interfered with through education, culture and belief systems, however it is possible with patience and persistence to rise above your present state. The work you are doing here is most effective when completed in a state of calm and of love.

Grief

One of the hardest parts of being human is when close connections, family and friends die. Within each culture, there are different practices, rituals and beliefs around the dead.

Let us talk a little about life, there is one certainty that the human body has a life expectancy, a period of measured time that it will live on earth. You have already learned and understood that you are a spiritual being having an earthly experience. That this experience, however short or long, is a training ground, an opportunity for growth, creativity and development for yourself and the collective.

The physical body is a vehicle of your spirit, a way in

which you can present yourself and your energy to the world. As your body develops through childhood and adolescence into maturity it carries all of the messages and learning with it. You have been working on the stories that your body carries that are limiting your life experience. The more you focus on decline in your maturity the quicker decline will be evident in your body. Maintaining youthfulness requires a healthy balanced life in mind, body and spirit, nutrition and exercise. Keep your mind active and stimulated and letting loose the old stories of 'retirement' and longevity.

Live everyday as if it were the last, as it may well be. Tell people you love them, honour them with your listening, honour them with your wisdom. Leave no trail of despair or hurt, solve your problems and create order in your life.

And live! Absorb every atom of love, creativity, joy and peace into your being throughout your life and you will have no regrets.

If sickness strikes, heal yourself by bringing peace to your mind and healing to your body. If something isn't working, meditate and imagine it working, if there is a density in your body see it shrinking, explore healthy options and alternative ways to heal alongside your physician's treatments.

If it is your time to leave: prepare yourself, prepare your loved ones, say your goodbyes and help them to understand that you will always be with them, when they call you, you will be there. Help children by telling them stories of wandering through the forest, climbing the highest mountain and how to shine their light. Show them how your light will remain and merge with theirs to bring hope and love to the world and teach them about life, love and all that you imagine life will be without this body.

It is a magical time, a time when words that were not spoken out of fear or lack of forgiveness can be aired. A time for healing and reminiscing, a time of reflection and storytelling. Take this final journey as a gift, a gift that you can give to those who will remain and help them to grieve gently and without fear. Communicate your needs, your wishes and choices for your transition and listen to what others desire for you. Share out your possessions with loved ones as a token of love and remembrance.

Surround yourself with all that you love, be it music, flowers, photographs or fabrics. Fill yourself with radiant golden light and release pain and discomfort, fill your room with the golden light of love that all who enter will feel the peace and beauty of this special time. Cry with those who cry and laugh with those who laugh and send your love out to all.

You will know when it's time to transition as you might hear the song of angels, or see visions of loved ones who come to accompany you, there might be a new light in your room, above you and even with your eyes closed you can sense the light calling you. As you take your final breath, your spirit will leave your body as you return to Love. You might find that you hover, do not delay your journey as there will be opportunity to provide care and succour to your loved ones when you are in All that Is.

When you leave earth and your body behind, you enter back as an energetic being into All that Is. You are greeted by your soul group and friends with great joy and celebration, you take time to assimilate in a space that you choose and over time, unpack all of your life experiences and explore the learning.

The passage of time in All that Is, is not measured as you measure it on earth and the time for reading through your records can take as long as you need. In All that Is, there is no judgement, there is only love. Whatever rules you broke on earth, whatever misdemeanours or transgressions you made, all of these are useful for collective understanding and development therefore there is nothing to fear.

On the subject of hell, the only hell is of your own making, in your mind. All souls return to All that Is without judgement for their mistakes, crimes or perceived sins.

Caring For The Dying

Your role has a mixture of practical tasks and emotional and spiritual support. The practical tasks include ensuring medical interventions are speedy, that your loved one is clean, comfortable and hydrated, risks to pressure areas are reduced and that they are pain free.

If they wish, a gentle massage of their body and or feet and hands will offer them relief if they are unable to walk. Toxins get caught up in the body and it can feel very painful and stiff. By offering this support they will feel loved and held. Take their lead in terms of their emotional and spiritual needs as written above and ensure that you are fully aware of their needs throughout their transition.

Give your loved one permission to transition, do not hold them back from their journey and however hard this is for you, engage your support systems to express your grief and emotions. If you find it helpful to write, write. Keep your focus on these last days with your loved one and make it as beautiful and healing as you can as this will help you in the next stage of your life.

Celebration Of Life

For all those who remain on earth, there is a sense of loss, unfulfilled hopes, dreams and plans and a concern for what life will be without your loved one. It is a time to be gentle with yourself, allowing all the feelings to rise within you, to filter through you and to release through tears, wailing or expressing your anger, hurt and loss. How you grieve is your choice, there is no right or wrong way, no order to follow or path to take. This is a personal and private experience unique to you and your relationship with the deceased. Take your time, examine all of those emotions until you are ready to face the world and begin your life without them.

Within your culture you will have rituals to follow, these are helpful in the grieving process, especially the paperwork that has to be completed and decisions made regarding the celebration of life or funeral. These activities draw people close together with one mission to say a formal goodbye to those that you love. Preparing the message of the legacy they leave behind and sifting through old photographs to honour their memory.

When the celebration of life is over and there is time to sit, bring yourself into Mystery. Follow the steps that work well for you and allow yourself to drift into that place where you are surrounded by love and support of the higher beings who guide you.

Do your best to find balance in your life, maintaining self care routines, eating well, walking in nature and meeting with loved ones to talk about your beloved and how you are feeling. Allow yourself to be in flow, not holding back your tears or screams, make sure that you have support to manage these times of freefall.

Journal, write your feelings down, let them flow, you will experience a whole range of emotions and if it helps to return to the list under Emotional Literacy and the process there, then use those as prompts to uncover all of your emotions.

IF you have responsibilities of children, business, pets, employment, do your best to negotiate time off and support with your family. By charging on with life and not dealing with your grief, you will hinder your progress which will present as physical illness and cause delays down the line.

Over time, you will find your balance again, you might be aware of your loved ones energy with you, call out to them and seek their counsel when you need it. Remember: There is nothing that separates us from Allthat IS and over time that will begin to feel real to you.

Maintaining Your Balance

Creating a state of calm and love on a daily basis with all of the opportunities for transformation that life offers is a goal that you will reach. Each step along this path will bring profound changes in your behavioural functioning and the relationships you form. You have learned many skills already which support your transformation and as you hone these, you will find that you are beginning to live a broader and deeper life experience. Maintaining balance when spinning the plates of life requires intention, commitment and discernment.

Simple Steps

Intention
Being completely clear about your goals, dreams, desires and plans and creating strategies to keep you on track. Sharing your intentions with key people in your life and holding yourself accountable for your own success. Scheduling time to review and evaluate your progress and remain flexible to account for inevitable changes in your life

Commitment
Daily dedication to the development of your goal through journal or writing. Guarding your language regarding your process when things aren't going smoothly and consistently bringing creative force and movement to your goal. Never faltering on your scheduled commitments by creative planning

Discernment
Being completely honest with yourself about motivation and drive and ensuring ethics and philosophy are based in Love. Being insightful when movement is haltered and remaining flexible and open to redirection. Seeking counsel and wisdom from others who are more knowledgeable than yourself. You are part of a collective, every step forward you take in the direction of your dream and the fulfilment of the goal impacts others. Including other people from the beginning, working in partnership and bouncing ideas will enhance your progress and this collective approach will also offer many viewpoints that will get you through stumbling blocks.

Choice
How you choose to live your life, to project to the world, to respond to the world will not be judged by All that Is. You are free to live the life you want. Make a choice every day about

how you will view the world and those who you meet.

Simple Steps

In the morning as you rise, take a few moments for gratitude. Thinking about the people in your life, the opportunities that are before you today, for all you will learn. Be on top of your day by knowing your schedule and who you will meet and be as prepared and organised as possible.

Make a decision or choice about how you will present to the world: Emotional state: I choose to be….. Calm, powerful, assertive etc. Physical state: I present as…… Confident, assured, knowledgeable. Mental state: I choose to be……..patient, tolerant and forgiving. Spiritual state: I choose to be………calm, peaceful and gentle.

At the end of the day reflect on all the learning and the choices you made. Plan for the day ahead, take time for yourself and enjoy restful sleep.

By making routines work for you, you will reduce fear based responses and reactions, you will feel on top of your life, all of which will improve your relationships, professional life and your sense of wellbeing.

Perception

How people see you is how they see you. On the journey of transformation you will begin to see life differently. The process of waking up to your own power will offer you a different perspective on life. Can you imagine that you are in a tall building, each floor of this building offers a different life perspective and experience. You were raised on floor 3 with all of its technology, philosophy, belief and education systems. It was a great foundation from which to grow, you loved your life but always had a sense that there was something more. Something more than your parents, community and culture could offer you.

You decided to travel outside of your community

and found other cultures with the same technology but different philosophies, beliefs and education. This widened your understanding and led to greater levels of curiosity and intention to find out what possibilities lay before you.

As you unpicked all of the beliefs and ideologies of your life, your urgency to discover more, that sense that there was more grew stronger and you decided to go through doors that you were told not to go through.

You were raised being told there was a danger in expanding your mind beyond the collective agreements. There were risks to relationships and opportunities on this 3rd floor. You were allowed to read the books from levels one and two - well at least some of them that agreed with the narrative of your culture but you were not allowed to go outside of this thinking.

You found a stairwell that led you up onto another level, you tentatively opened the door that said level 5. As the door cracked open, the light was brighter than you had ever seen, it was pure golden light and the scent that came through the door was fresh and pure, like the smell of a flower that you didn't recognise.

As you walked into the large open space, it was clear and calm, the space seemed to stretch on for miles and you could see fields of flowers and fruits growing and buildings that moulded into the landscape. As your eyes adjusted to the light you began to see shapes, people, beings who moved so gently it was as if they were floating. These people were radiant with golden light and were guiding you through the hallways of this beautiful space. They led you to a room with soft furnishings and brought you a drink of the freshest water you had ever tasted.

Time passed as these beings sat with you and answered all of your questions. They spoke gently and calmly, you felt wrapped in the love that was here. They asked if you would like to go to school to learn more about life at this vibration and you eagerly said yes.

As you walked gently through the hallways of this space you wondered what it was called and who you would meet here. You arrived at the school, which was unlike anything you had seen before. There were circles of beings collecting together playing with ideas and technologies you had not seen before. You joined in a circle with the guide and felt completely at home as they welcomed you and created space for you. They were considering a plant that was sitting on the floor, it was unlike any plant you had seen before and they explained that it was a plant for healing planet earth. They were extracting its energy and moulding it into different shapes to watch how it corrected itself. You were fascinated as it seemed that both the plant and the beings were talking to each other, in complete harmony and with a shared intention of understanding and creative development.

As the school dispersed your guide took you to another room, a room with records of life. Your book was opened on a table before you and you both went through the stories of your lives. How you had been a carpenter, a mother, a musician, a philosopher, a prisoner and a soldier.

You had no knowledge of these lives or the learnings you had received throughout these lives which lead you to now. You began to understanding that the seeds of your passions were already planted in you, your love for wood, music, reading, your hatred of war and hardship - all of these seeds were here in the very heart of you and now that you understood why they are there, you began to understand why you chose this life, these parents and all that the community could offer.

With this new knowledge and this deep connection you found at this level, you began to know an ease in your heart, mind and spirit. This brought a deep sense of calm and freedom and also an urgency in you to begin the process of sharing this knowledge with people on your level.

Your guide smiled and led you back to the door that you first came through, they gave you a key, a golden key that was not made of metal or anything solid, and you placed it in your heart. They told you this key allowed you eternal access to this level and that you can visit any time you wish. Your heart was light and your mind free now and you embraced your guide and left.

As you descended to the third floor, you noticed you were back in your own clothes but you still radiated that pure golden light. You now knew your mission, your service and began to feel completely empowered without any fear.

You had climbed the highest mountain, reached the next level, understood how the limiting of the human experience had been created through indoctrination and fear and were ready now for the greater part of your journey.

And now it's time to rest, to rest in all that you have learned and fill yourself with lovelight whilst Resting in Shallow Waters.

RESTING IN SHALLOW WATER

Amidst all the transformation in this journey, the stages and steps you have taken and will continue to take throughout your life, now is your time to Be.

Making time for the inner work outside of the conscious mind to gently and lovingly maintain flow and to be fully engaged in your connection to All that Is.

INTRODUCTION
Ⓟ5:1

I am taking you on a journey to a magical place where the air is clear and the light that shines upon it highlights sparkles of energy that emanate from all living beings. The rocks and the stones, the very earth you stand on is alive and sparkling with the light of love.

You wander down a well trodden path and hear the earth moving to support your footsteps, you can see the flowers leaning in to you, to observe your magnificence and to merge with your energy. You are feeling lighter and more joyful with every step.

The path leads on and although you don't recognise this place, it feels familiar, you look down at your bare feet and they are glowing with golden light, you're wearing a floating robe that shines as if it were studded with diamonds and you can see that you are shining brighter and brighter with every step.

The trees are hanging low with magnificent fruits and flowers, wild, wonderful and free and you reach out and ask the tree if you can eat one of its fruits. The tree leans forward and brings a branch towards you. The fruit leans in and you pluck it from its branch, it is the most beautiful fruit you have ever seen. You hold it, stroke it, smell it and then release its wonder into you. With each bite you begin to feel more and more alive, it is as if the fruit is living in you, wild, fresh and free.

There's a skip in your step as you carry on in this magnificent landscape. You notice creatures and insects along the way, going about their business of living and as you walk by it's as if they notice you and acknowledge your presence.

Before you, there is a waterfall and you wander towards it led by the path and the sound of rushing water. The air is filled with droplets and you open your mouth drink this magnificent fresh pure water. As you reach the waterfall you can see that the path leads underneath it. Walking around the deepest blue pool with frogs, toads, fish and plants with insects buzzing in the frenzy of the waterfall bubbles and splashes, you imagine what it might be like to share their experience.

You wander onwards towards the fall, which is louder now and more vibrant and energetic than you have ever experienced before. The energy seems to enter into you and you find a strength that is surprising and somewhat overwhelming at this moment. You cry and let out residue feelings of shame, hurt and lack, knowing that your power is now free to hold, to explore and to become.

Behind the waterfall the path leads into a cave, the air is cool and the walls wet with eternal splashing. The rocks are smooth under your bare feet and you walk with ease and strength into the vast chasm of this cave. There is a light here, not from the sun, the light is in the very rocks. A small pool glistens, the water appears as liquid gold and you wander around this space looking to see where the path leads.

You feel compelled to look at the inscriptions on the walls, hieroglyphs and symbols mixed with drawings of animals and beings. These seem familiar as you read their stories and decide to rest on a rock and enjoy this wonderful cool golden cave.

You drift into a wonderful sleep and dream of diving into the golden pond where the water is so fresh and welcoming. You dream that you swim down deep underground and discover that you can breathe underwater.

You find yourself at the bottom of the pond where there is a stream that leads both in front and behind, you cannot decide which way to go. You take a moment just hovering there looking up to where you are sleeping and connect to your intuition, you swim forwards, the stream becomes narrower and as you continue you find that your body has become smaller to ease your path, then the stream opens up to the pond that you had walked by with frogs, toads, fish and insects playing in the water. You explore this magical underwater world and now know what it feels like to share their experience and as you swim they lean into you and acknowledge your presence.

You wake from your dream in this beautiful golden cavern and there before you is the pathway that leads home.

When you are living in harmony, abundance flows towards you, life has treasured moments that make your heart sing. Being in presence, fully aware of everything around you and engaging in the magic and wonder of life will serve through all of the twists and turns of life on earth.

WATER

Water is one of the best conductors of the spirit. It enables you to float, to flow, to gently cleanse the mind and the body.

When you are in a deep state of calm, where the deep silence lives, where your mind is at rest and you feel at one with the world. This is when you are metaphorically resting in shallow water.

The river of life is winding, there are shallows, deep waters, waterfalls, brooks and streams. Learning to navigate these natural ebbs and flows of life requires a commitment to peace, love and tranquillity.

You have learned so much already about yourself and your spiritual connection, you have practised rituals that enable you to reach the shallow waters.

And it is within these shallow waters where you can explore intentions, work out possible futures, begin the process of understanding yourself, your reactions and your stumbling blocks, recognising your own strengths and areas for growth, you will use this powerful time to dream the life you love.

Dreamtime Ⓟ5:2

Do you have a dream, a goal, a vision of the future
when you have everything in place? Dreaming
something into being requires focus, commitment and
intention, will you dream with me for a while?

Imagine that you are standing before a large crowd, dressed in elegant clothes and shining like the sun. Your audience awaits your wisdom with great anticipation and

143

there is a loud hum in the room as they chat to each other.

Silence falls as you are introduced to the crowd, loud applause welcomes you to centre stage. In power and confidence you hold the attention of the room, sharing your wisdom and engaging the audience with your charismatic wit and oratory skills.

You tell them your story of the experiences you had and the emotions that ruled you. You tell them the key points on your journey up to this moment in time standing there on the stage. You show them the steps you took and tell them stories which would have sounded unbelievable to you in the past, but there you are and the audience is eating up every word.

You complete your talk and notice the audience, they are entranced by your words, you know that some people absorb every word and for others it was unbelievable and too challenging but you smiled and thank them. The audience come to life and give you a standing ovation, you leave the stage with a glow in your heart.

Take time to reflect on this imaginary YOU, of course not everyone is destined for a large audience, some might write books, poems, letters, others might record their experiences in a daily journal, however we tell our story, it needs to be heard.

Visioning

When you are resting in shallow water, the stream of life is showing you the way, use some of this time to dream of the future you desire. Start with small things and imagine that you already have these, seeing how they might transform your life, how they might serve others. Notice all that you need to notice and bring to life your needs one by one. Create unlimited visions and give yourself permission to be expansive, to reach far beyond any goal you might have set, to stretch your imagination as far as it can go.

When you allow this great stream of consciousness to

come through you, it will bring power to your life. If after experiencing these visions you challenge all that you created in your mind, use these challenging thoughts as a creative force to propel you in the direction of your vision.

Consider all of the inventors that have gone before, they started off with a vision and after trial upon trial, failure upon failure, they did not give up, they could 'see it' and they reached out until they found it. Be as intentional and committed to your goals as they were and you will find your way.

Breathwork

Possibly one of the most powerful tools you have in your toolkit, is housed inside of you. You are gaining more control over this power, each time you go into mystery.

There is magic in your breath and you can manipulate it to create different vibrations within your body: As you expand your breath, you will raise your energy creating changes in your body chemistry and brain activity that prepare you for the next challenge.

As you slow your breath it amplifies compassion and peace within your heart centre and the love codes there are energised and rise through you and out into the world. With focussed attention and intention, you can take your breath to higher levels of vibrational energy, which connects the light that shines within and your connection through the golden thread.

Ensure your breathing pattern is slow and gentle, extend your outbreath a little and remain in this space, allowing your imagination to flood you with golden light, to raise you to a state of magnificence. You might choose to bring the radiant golden light from earth through your spine and see it radiating around the world.

Create imagery that enhances your experience, listen to subtle music that can only be heard in this space and notice gentle scents wafting through the air. Get lost in the imagery and experience until you are at one with All that Is.

You might feel like you are floating as your energy rises and any sense of discomfort might be forgotten in these moments. This is a perfect state for healing yourself of angst, concerns or mental and physical health issues. Remember that in the connection to All that Is, you have access to higher powers, ascended masters, spirit guides and loved ones and we are all here to serve you.

Your breath is simply an access door to spirit, inspiration is to bring in the spirit and like all doors it opens up to new opportunities. It inspires you to be in connection and flow with the universe, it inspires you to notice everything around you, to become one with all, it inspires you to create: to create magic, miracles, healing, artwork and a deeper sense of self. In this gentle breath you are in complete power and control and can use this to manage times when you feel less than powerful.

As you rest in shallow waters, you find that gentle place of flow which allows you to realign with your truth and your natural energetic frequency. Life was never meant to be this hard, when you stand in your truth in the shallows, where you can breathe, you will find that standing up for your right to challenge all you were told before, becomes manageable. However, like all skills they take practice, therefore the more time you spend here, the more you understand how to use your breath to your benefit, the more you will be able to stay calm with a sense of wellbeing and power in more troubled waters.

Award yourself time every day to get to know your breath, your flow, your alignment, then you will begin to experience a power and peace beyond your imagination. Placing your palms on your heart centre whilst practising your breathwork will heighten the experience as well as helping you maintain focus. Taking breathwork to the next level, you can begin the practice of healing yourself.

Simple Steps   Ⓟ5:3

A meditation on the breath for calm and compassion: Gather your time and tools and make space in your body and mind for this practice:

As you sit and make your body comfortable, notice any thoughts that are in your mind and process what you can before allowing them to drift off. Feel the cloth on your skin, notice the warmth of the air around you and gently rub your palms together in circular motion. With each rotation focus on the sensations this brings and any thoughts that pop up. Notice what you are doing with your breath and use this stroking with soft, gentle yet full breaths into the lower belly. With your eyes closed watch your hands move from right to left.

Maintain this rhythm of hands, eyes and breath until you feel that warm sense of calm you seek. Now cross your arms and rest your hands on your upper arms, keep them still as your body finds its comfort again. Now gently tap your arms, right then left, in rhythm with your breath whilst watching with your eyes. Notice how you feel, the rhythm of your breath and the warmth of your body.

We are going on a journey alongside a beck where a gentle stream of water glistens in the dappled shade of willows. There are fish in the water following your path, you can see the insects flying, dandelion seed heads floating in the air and everything feels like it is happening in slow motion.

You are dressed in an offwhite gown with bare feet, the ground is soft and gentle and the sun is warming your skin. Your senses are heightened and you can hear the fish blowing bubbles, the insects landing on the water and leaves rustling in the gentle breeze. You can smell the grass, the bark of the trees, the scent of wild flowers and the earth beneath your feet. The air is clear and the skies are crisp with gentle clouds barely moving before you.

You spy a rainbow in the distance as you walk towards the field of red and gold. When you reach the field you sit with your feet in the stream and rest your head back on a clump of soft grass. As the water laps your feet, you enter into Mystery, where you meet your guide, who takes you on a magical journey through the years, showing you all the love you have received. You take note of all those opportunities where you didn't feel loved, yet love was all around you, you notice the smiles, the touch on the arm, the hugs, you remember unexpected gifts and cards and feel warmed and blessed by all the love you have received.

Your guide then shows you the times where you have given love and compassion to loved ones, strangers, colleagues and neighbours. You notice the times when you had not recognised the impact your kindness had on the receiver and your heart is full.

Your guide then rises with you high above the earth and shows you all the love that is flowing through the air, through nature, through humans and these wisps of gold thread look like a beautiful tapestry, you are bursting with love and gratitude for this moment.

The fear that had been residing in you pops out like a cork from a shaken bottle of champagne and you feel free. It is true that love wins the day, you can see the contrasting threads of fear and pain, dwarfed by the beauty of the golden threads.

You cannot help but take a deep and gentle full breath with the power of this imagery and then you find yourself back in your space at home. You are overflowing with calm, peace and compassion for those who are fearful and you cross your arms again, as if holding the world and you tap your arms filling all creation with love.

Use this meditation any time you are feeling out of alignment with your true nature and All that Is.

Simple Steps   Ⓟ5:4

A Meditation to 'let go' of limiting thoughts. Sit quietly to settle your body into the space, allow your thoughts to float around without concern.

When you are at peace: Imagine you are standing near a powerful waterfall with the energy of the water falling and splashing around you, you can feel the spray and sense the power of the fall. You notice that your breath is picking up the rhythm of the fall and as you stand there mesmerised by the powerful beauty of this space, with the moisture on your face. Bring to mind that thought that will not leave you, assign a colour, word or image to this thought. Then bring to mind the desired state you imagine you will experience once you have 'let go' and once again assign a colour, word or image.

Sit with both images for a while to regain your poise. Now, focus on your breath until you are breathing slow, full and in a gentle rhythm. On your next full breath in, bring to mind the thought that will not let you go, let it in with your breath using the colour, word or image and then as you breathe out, imagine that the colour, word or image is leaving and being caught up in the mist of the waterfall. Repeat until you can no longer find that thought.

Now, bring in the desired state through colour, word or image and allow it to restore and nourish you with every breath, filling each cell of your body whilst allowing the flow of air to find its rhythm and you might notice your vibration rising with each breath.

As you assimilate these changes continue to enjoy being in the presence of this powerful energy as the river runs its course and flows ever onwards to the sea. In the knowledge that you too are in flow, learning, evolving and growing in power and strength.

Balance & Strength   Ⓟ5:5

This stream of life comes to you and through you and as you find your balance and strength there is a need for great self care. You are channelling universal love at all times, picking up energies and cleansing them whilst running your own life with all of its expectations.

It is possible that your awareness of other energies

around you might lead to feeling depleted, exhausted, burnt out and depressed. You can prevent this by resting in shallow water. What image does that conjure up for you? What feelings does it generate within you? Where are those feelings? What colour are they?

Imagine now, a warm and beautiful place, with a river running through it, a wide river with gentle banks, with reeds and rivulets running into it. If you were to float up, high above the river you would see it meandering across the land with gentle waterfalls leading to fast running waters and returning again to meandering gently through the land.

Notice all the activity from this bird's eye view and look back along the river from where you came. Can you see the twists and turns, the boulders, the fast waters where life felt out of control and the peaceful river when you found your balance?

There is much to learn from the twists and turns of life and when you have learned all you need, float back down into your body and enjoy the gentle lapping of the waters, as you rest at the edge in the shallows. Here you can stay for a while, focus attention on your breath and enter into mystery.

Giving yourself this time to connect to the source of all that is, like an infusion of love and healing, imagine the golden thread entering into and surrounding you with golden light, bask here in that feeling of being completely at one with your soul energy, draw all that you need from here and listen to your heart's longing and souls guidance. You can rest here as long as you need.

Highest Wisdom

As you grow more and more familiar with your highest wisdom, you will discover their voice and you may find out their name. The more time you spend with your soul energy the less fear and concern disturb your path and the more you are able to stride out in confidence as a spiritual being in a physical body.

The more comfortable you get with this practice, the

more you open yourself to further mysteries of the universe. Your understanding of life and all its beauty grows and you find that you can float above drama and criticism. Your capacity to love and forgive grows as you stop taking things personally and observe everything with curiosity and genuine interest.

You can gain more support from All that Is and link into the mystery of many souls that you have known, heard of or read about. For example when you are faced with a practical dilemma or a healing dilemma you can call out for assistance, if you have an accounting problem you might ask for an accountant to guide you. Higher powers, ascended masters, spirit guides and loved ones are all here to serve you.

Your breath is simply an access door to spirit, inspiration is to bring in the spirit and like all doors it opens up to new opportunities. It inspires you to be in connection and flow with the universe, it inspires you to notice everything around you, to become one with all, it inspires you to create: to create magic, miracles, healing, artwork and a deeper sense of self. In this gentle breath you are in complete power and control and can use this to manage times when you feel less than powerful.

As you rest in shallow waters, you find that gentle place of flow which allows you to realign with your truth and your natural energetic frequency. Life was never meant to be this hard, when you stand in your truth in the shallows, where you can breathe, then you will find that standing up for your rights to challenge all you were told becomes manageable. However, like all skills they take practice, therefore the more time you spend here, the more you understand how to use your breath to your benefit, the more you will be able to stay calm with a sense of wellbeing and power in more troubled waters.

Award yourself time every day to get to know your breath, your flow, your alignment, then you will begin to experience a power and peace beyond your imagination. Placing your palms on your heart centre whilst practising your breathwork will heighten the experience as well as helping you maintain focus. Taking breathwork to the next level, you can begin the practice of healing yourself.

Simple Steps

Decide your need and intention and enter into mystery.
Ask for support naming the need. Whilst focussing on your
breath listen for any guidance, you might be called to write
whilst your guides dictate, or just to write your thoughts
down without cross checking, just letting the ink flow.
Remain here until there is peace about the need and maybe
a direction. Open your eyes and go back to your needs and
explore new ways to tackle the issue.

The Stream

Can you imagine a stream, a gentle brook, clear water, filled
with life, gently travelling through clean land, unpopulated,
fresh and untouched by man's hands? A watering place for
creatures who live quietly in peace and harmony, who fill
their days with freedom to roam without fear. Yes there are
predators and yes there are losses, but day by day there is a
life to live without concern about a possible future.

Imagine there was such a place for you to visit,
without need to change it, just to become one with it. Loving
the light and sounds here and filling your days with gentle
thoughts and observations. Picking the wild plants and
berries for sustenance and drinking from the pure waters of
the stream, a place of pure peace.

Imagine that there are others who visit you here,
offering kind words, reflections and encouragement, and at
times words that cut straight to the heart of the matter
without pain and as swift as a surgeon's knife, the limitation
is removed.

This is the vision you can create when you are resting
in shallow waters. Here you are creating space to make a
powerful connection to your highest potential, your mystery
and your guides. It is here in this space where the true magic

is fully realised, it is here that you find your truth, your gifts and your purpose.

On the spiritual path there is much learning and much delving into the unknown aspect of self. Bringing all your feelings and thoughts to a sacred space without judgement where you meet only love, will help you to find a new lens to look at your past, present and future.

You have many parts, roles you play, lenses you look through,. If you are the 'boss at work' are you the 'boss at home'? You play these roles to expand who you are and your capacity, the more familiar you are with all aspects of self, the more easily you will glide from one role to another.

What makes for a smooth life is when the core of you is sustained, irrespective of the role you play. Your essence is strong, morales are clear, judgments suspended and expectations are focussed on your own responsibility for health and wellbeing. You look through the eyes of love first, then if necessary for scrutiny, look through the eyes of discernment.

The art of listening with this core strength, enables you to magically read people, enabling you to read between the words and the lines, seeing their true nature and needs. Then within your capacity the words you speak will be crystal clear and healing for the other.

It is here in this quiet sacred space that you can develop your skills, you can listen to the sounds of your body, become aware of any areas of discomfort, use your power of healing to relieve distress and fill your body with the light of love. Infused, immersed, bringing with it a peace that is beyond understanding and a calm in the breath and the heart.

It is here you can amplify other tools you have learned throughout the years, investigating their capacities and modifying your understanding to enhance the power of these tools. The power of intuition here is amplified and if this is new to you,here is a good place to gain affirmation of what you intuit.

A Simple Exercise

You can increase intuition by physically opening your third eye by gently massaging between your eyebrows and using three fingers on both hands gently stroking from the middle of your forehead upwards and then across towards your temples with your eyes closed. If you feel blocked then stroke alternate sides in a gentle rhythm .

You can increase your capacity to hear what is said and unsaid by a simple stroking of your head around your ears using all your fingers with cupped hands, again if you feel blocked massage alternate sides in a gentle rhythm.

Getting to know your own body is the most powerful way to build your skills to share your gifts as a healer if that is your desired path.

When I was on earth, I worked with people who were entrenched in fear, they couldn't think straight because they believed some dark force was going to curse them and all whom they loved. Their minds were contaminated and their bodies were sick because of this. Keeping your mind free of fear is paramount on the spiritual path. This is where the power of discernment can be engaged instead of the fear response.

In a life and death situation, your responses are heightened by your spiritual connection to All that Is and you will react with a calmness that will amaze. You will be working at a multidimensional level as you call in your guides and the power of the universe to provide you with the support you need whilst finding a core strength that is amplified at that time. Your mind will be on the prevention of catastrophe rather than fear. You will see a solution and do your best to achieve a positive outcome. Should catastrophe strike and others do not survive, you will have a core strength that will support your own recovery.

THE MAGIC OF SILENCE

There is so much noise, it is hard to escape the noise of life, the electronic buzzing, the bombardment of colour, light and sound. This can be exhausting, even sleep is full of sounds and sights, as you process your day, it is only in the deepest sleep where you are still.

Will you make a commitment to yourself to find your silence? Will you take time each day to stop the noise, the colours, the demands and the feelings? Can you find a place in the world where the only sounds are that of nature, birdsong, trees rustling, waves lapping, streams bubbling?

Can you sit there, alone, unhurried without expectation allowing yourself this time to BE? Settle yourself into mystery in that space. Can you allow those words running through your head to fade away and drift into a space of nothing, allowing as long as it takes to get there, leaning into the silence and breathing out slowly, breathing in only when charged to breathe, gentle yet full breaths?

Here in the silence, you can meet your heart's desire, your purpose, your soul connection. Here in the silence you can create a world, a reality where all you dream of being is realised. You can try on magnificence, experiment with feeling amazing, powerful, invincible or magical. Here in this space no questions require answers, there is only love and you are drenched in it and feel completely at ease.

Here you can create; powerful creator that you are and however you choose to bring to life your creations, it is here in the silence that they are first created. You can bring thoughts about certain people into this space, people who you want to heal, people who you want to get to know, people who you want to forgive.

The more time you spend here, the more creative you will become. The more peace you experience here, the more peaceful you will be amongst all the noise and colours of life. IF you are crazy busy in life, then take time to be in silence in order that you can manage the business of your day.

Bringing Silence Into Your Day To Day Life

The people you meet day by day need silence in their lives too. Look for ways to bring silence in your home, your work and your play. Turn off the noise, the electronic buzz, the bright colours. Sit with people actively listening, learn to read between the lines and without need to speak.

Invite people to sit with you if they are experiencing anxiety, shock or grief. Just sit with them, holding space for them. Light a candle for them to direct their focus, give them a crystal to hold and a glass of refreshing water to drink. Silently, hold them in your heart, hold their hand or shoulder if they need that. Look deep into their hearts and bring that Golden Thread through you to their need, see them filling with Radiant Golden Light and being healed. Speak softly, gently, lovingly and they will feel held.

Daily: sit quietly, mindfully watching the clouds in the sky or watching the spaces between the branches of a tree. Turn off electronic devices and eat in silence, slowly, gratefully enjoying each bite, the taste, the texture and nourishment.

Sit around the table with your family and friends, mixing silence with the sharing stories of the day, listening and encouraging each other, laughing and planning. Play games together and work together, bumping into each other in activity, without need for noise, or talking. Just enjoying the playfulness of connection.

Here in the silence, you will find harmony, peace and

creativity.

Using Silence To Enter Into Mystery

Silent meditation is a place of deep mystery. When you are learning to meditate, you might find guidance is useful and you might add music, or binaural sounds to support you to get into a meditative state, a daydream trance state. The more experienced you become will enable you to enter into mystery through the breath and into silence.

Here in this deeper state of mystery, you can bring your intentions and expand your experience. This is more advanced work for you to experience.

Simple Steps   ℗5:6

As you prepare for mystery, bring to mind a concern: We will use the example of 'a world issue'. In conscious awareness, highlight the solution you seek - be it peaceful resolution, safety for people, rainfall to dampen bush fires etc. Please choose from current issues of concern

Allow yourself to go into mystery through the breath, the golden thread and the radiant golden light. Deepen your experience using imagination to conjure images of your concern. Imagine yourself only as a bright light. Imagine that you bring your bright light into the midst of the concern, see yourself standing there. Hold the light here and observe it, with every breath expand your light to cover the issue of concern and pour love deep into every area you can reach.

Notice any density leaving the area of concern, you might see this as dark energy rising, or in the case of a bush fire, droplets of rain dampening the flames.

Stay with this meditation for as long as you are able, creating the solution you seek in your imagination. If you wish, invite guides, angels and beings to support you in your task.

As you pull your light back into your body and begin the process of returning to this space, trust that the work you have done is complete and that others will take over. Do not let the density of this issue weigh heavy on you, as you need to maintain your vibrational energy of love to raise the whole planet. Take time to realign yourself, drink water and write in your journal

Managing Contrast Peacefully

Life will throw many opportunities in your path. Each of these are there to support your journey - even the ones that you find unpleasant or uncomfortable. By reframing this as contrast, you enable understanding and growth.

When you stop judging each experience as either good, bad or indifferent, then the world of contrast is opened. Without contrast there is little shape to this world. You need light to appreciate the dark and vice versa. Life is full of shades, shadows and dark spaces, this is how you know the light.

An Example

You fail to achieve your expectation, maybe an exam, an interview or a new opportunity. You had set high hopes on success and had seen all the possibilities that would arise from it. You are disappointed and all of those old limiting stories come forth, not as strong as before because you have worked on them. But nevertheless, the memory floods back and it sets you onto an old path of self-deprecating commentary.

Immediately; because you know where this path ends, how dark, lonely and lifeless it is, you choose to 'change your state' by an acknowledgement that you have not achieved your expectations and a decision to work on those feelings, but for now you will rise above this and do something different.

You go for a quick walk in nature, looking up into the sky, expressing gratitude and love for everything in your life. Then you set a time to process the disappointment and let it go whilst you get on with living.

Simple Steps   ℗5:7

Processing disappointment: Award yourself time to rest in shallow waters. Acknowledge your feelings about the disappointment. Take a full and gentle breath into your belly and make yourself comfortable. Give all the feelings that rise in you time to express themselves, without judgement until you are spent.

Gently guide yourself back into your breath and relax into your body, asking for support and guidance from your highest wisdom and guides. In your imagination, rise out of your body and hover above yourself, notice everything around you and look for the path leading forwards. See how it twists and turns and then leads into a light and open space full of opportunity.

Breathe in this possible future and then look for the path that you would have traversed had you achieved success. Notice where it led and learn from it, absorbing all you need to know, then drift back down into your body and notice any sensations & feelings that remain.

Bring a ball of radiant golden light into your body and imagine it collecting all sensations and feelings and transmuting them into calm and peaceful energy. An energy that acknowledges Everything is in Perfect Order and stay in mystery until you are completely at peace and ease.

On the spiritual path you are living in harmony with your highest wisdom, the all knowing aspect of you. Each chapter of your life offers contrasting situations that enable your growth and some of these are stepping stones towards the work you intended to do here on earth: your purpose. There is an understanding and acceptance that you have free will and you may or may not choose to fulfil those intentions.

When Another Offers Contrast

The human experience is fraught with ego squabbles, these are perfect opportunities for growth and often result in setting the other free to walk their path. Depending which aspect of you holds the power, will depend on how you generate ego squabbles.

Can you let love be your highest power? And thus allow ego its rightful place? When you choose to look through the lens of love, you can set people free without drama or misunderstanding.

Simple Steps

You find yourself in a conflicting situation with another:
Diffuse the situation: Listen to everything the other is saying, read between the lines, read body language and allow the other person to vent until they are spent. Maintain a neutral expression and posture.

Whilst they are speaking: Fill them with the light of love and encase them in a ball of Radiant Golden Light. Imagine that all of the angst is rising out of them and you are able to listen to their heart to discover the real issue?

When it is your time to speak: "I hear what you are saying, I am sorry for my part in this, I am sorry that my actions have caused you distress. Can we sit down and talk about how to move forward from here?"

Allow the other to speak their truth and remember:
Love does not take accusation personally. Love sees every opportunity for growth. Acknowledge your faults and the unhealed part of you. Know that the other is operating from their unhealed parts too.

Seek resolution: Through forgiveness not blame, through honesty not deceit and through Love. This may take practice, but this is the path of peace and the more work you do on your own unhealed parts, the more opportunities will come your way to hold up a mirror to show you the way.

When you are truly grateful for your life, everything and everybody in it, then you will find that you can rest peacefully. When you meet up with others who are out of alignment with you and are showing you contrast, check whether you have some work to do. Use these opportunities wisely and be grateful for those that support your growth. After all these people may be part of your soul group and have contracted with you to show you the way.

CREATING BALANCE

Imagine that you are the fulcrum on the scales of your life, no longer rising or falling with the events that present themselves, you are stable and firmly planted in understanding of yourself.

To become the fulcrum requires much time resting in shallow waters. It is here that you give yourself the time and attention you need to find out exactly who you are. With all the steps and stages you have taken already, unveiling the light that shines from you, the layers of limitation, belief, culture and the stories that you told yourself, you are really beginning to discover your intrinsic nature.

When you dedicate time to yourself, your growth, development and understanding, you will speed the process of living a balanced life. Resting in shallow waters is the place where you decide to do this work. It might mean a daily practice, or a regular planned retreat where you can find time unhindered to go within, to pamper yourself, to rest in nature, to write and to dream.

Turning off the noise of life is a simple step to take, even if this means rising before the children awake, to give yourself time to listen to your heart.

What Are Your Needs?

Without judgement or measure: Give yourself permission to honestly say what you need, want and would like. And in contrast, without judgement: Give yourself permission to say "I don't want, I'm struggling, I don't like."

Contrast gives great opportunity for growth and by

discovering what you don't want will reveal more layers of your story and help you to know more clearly what you do want.

When you spend time in quiet solitude, exploring your needs, desires, dreams and goals you grow, the speed of growth through epiphanies, and visions enable you to begin to know yourself as the powerful magnificent soul that you are.

It is only through knowing yourself that you can live a true and balanced life. Knowing yourself is a place of acceptance of the essence of who you are, it may be that one of your key gifts or skills is the antithesis of your culture, education or belief system. Is this why you have always felt out of balance, as if you didn't belong?

Coming to terms with your true essence, aligns you with your soul energy enabling you to match the pure vibration of love that emanates through you via the Golden Thread.

When you are resting in shallow water, there is no fear of drowning or being carried by the tide, you are completely safe to explore all of these aspects of who you are. To find ways to be comfortable with yourself and give yourself permission to be.

Strength

You have considered the power of the ego, which is there to serve you, to support and guide your understanding and to protect you. But when you give your power away to the ego, it plays a very different game.

You will know people who are power hungry, whose egos have been given reign. Where self-esteem has risen beyond the point of love to self-serving activity lacking in compassion, concern or love for the collective. If you notice this trait in yourself, all is not lost, you can reign your ego back in and find your balance.

Take time resting in shallow water to fully examine the events that led to your ego taking over personal power, then once you understand the story, use the many tools in your toolkit to manage and dissolve the story to set yourself free.

Then take your time to bring love into the scenarios that require attention and be guided in the path to resolution. You might have given your power over to emotions, feelings, diagnosis, story, victim or experiences. It is not unusual and you are not alone.

Take your time to come to terms with your present and make headway in bringing peace back into your life. You are not defined by your past, you are defined by your actions that bring you back to love. Most often Fear is the root to the Ego takeover, it may or may not relate to this life experience, it could be that you observed another's actions and it impacted on your life.

Trauma, observed or experienced can reduce your strength, that core strength that you brought to this life can be damaged as fear is allowed to reign. This fear is self generating and as it takes over, strength diminishes. Leaving you vulnerable and unable to take back control. Take steps today to find your peace and restore your power.

Simple Steps   Ⓟ5:8

Take yourself into mystery: Put your hands on your heartspace and fill yourself with golden light through the golden thread then fill yourself with radiant golden light from earth.

Surround yourself, the space you are in and under your feet with the golden light of love until you are in complete peace. Ask one of your guides to witness your process. Bring to mind the event, witnessed or experienced , your picture doesn't need detail. Take your hands cupped in front of you and imagine that you can place the event in your hands. Imagine the event as if in a snowglobe, fill it with all the imagery and feelings you can then hand the globe to your guide.

As they hold it, see if you can notice anything that

links you to the event and then take your power & strength back. You can do this by speaking out loud, in your head or by reaching out and breaking any links. As you do this, notice the image beginning to fade as the people, the images, the feelings slowly disappear and watch as the snow globe fills with blue light. Notice how it swirls and clears and imagine that you can see the blue light rise high up into the atmosphere to carry all the pain and memory to source energy in All that Is to be cleansed and healed.

Your guide places their hands on your shoulders, you feel a vibration throughout your body as your strength returns. Sit until you have assimilated all you have learned and return to presence and rest in shallow waters until you are ready to resume your day.

Pride

In the process of unveiling the magic of you, there is a realisation of your worth and value, you are discovering your gifts and the importance of your existence. Self image, self worth, self respect and self esteem are all positive aspects of living a spiritual life in the human experience. Knowing yourself and loving yourself are powerful ways to live on earth.

With this knowledge you find your strength and a personal power that is gentle, kind, calm and compassionate. Life will begin to flow and others begin to witness your transformation. Relationships are easier now as you have learned not to take things personally, you know that Everything is in Perfect Order and difficulties arise out of fear filled responses and that love is the antidote to fear.

You have also found the strength to make healthier choices in relationships, as you consider the impact you are having upon each other and seek functional ways to support growth. You will find that the wounds that once limited you are healing and the language you use is changing and is now less judgemental, kinder and more understanding of your own and others foibles.

Strength is presented as confidence wrapped up in kindness, you are able to communicate your strength without the other feeling inferior or under control and in all walks of your life, you are being noticed for your personal power.

Pride is showing up as self respect and as you build this loving relationship with yourself, you are finding yourself able to assert your needs in gentle and loving ways. Great pleasure and satisfaction is found in small wins throughout each day and the more you experience, the more is attracted to you.

The Path Of Peace, Love & Tranquillity

Every day on the spiritual path, you dedicate yourself to further growth and learning, curious of each event, exchange and the unexpected. There seems to be a message and opportunity for learning in everything and life becomes exciting.

Commitment to your path is eased when you find a routine that works well for you, a time dedicated to your breath to healing and to peace. Each day filling yourself with the Golden Light of Love and letting go of experiences, memories and thoughts that limit your journey.

When you are impacted by the news, community, loved ones, disappointments and situations that create risk, there will be a greater need to find your balance again.

When you have made the commitment to the path of peace, love and tranquillity and find yourself in chaos and confusion because of life circumstances. Create a space within your busy day to bring yourself back to calm.

Hold your emotions and feelings until you are alone, when you can then give yourself permission to explore them, by allowing your feelings room, you can extract all that you need to from an explosion of emotion and recognise where fear has crept in.

The more you explore now, the easier it will be to manage pervading issues, sit without judgement and allow the feelings to flow until they are spent and you can breathe again.

Once the feelings are back under your control, then you can begin to unravel the information you have received and examine it from many angles. Take as long as you need with this process, diligence will pay off here. Work out what you feel, why you feel it and what the best route is for you. Look for ways to communicate what you are feeling and make decisions about actions you will take.

Once back in the situation, be aware of your communication and reactions, it is easy to get caught up in the drama of different situations and fall into the 'angst trap'. Look for ways to find your peace again, fill yourself with the golden light of love and support any others affected.

When you are alone and can enter into mystery, provide yourself with time and comfort to complete your process and find your balance.

A Meditation For Tranquillity   Ⓟ5:9

You are sitting on a park bench with the sun streaming through the trees, your space is cool enough to be comfortable and you are enjoying the comings and goings of the people here. Out in the distance you can see one of your favourite landmarks, a place where you go to whenever you can, but for now, in the midst of a busy day, you are here, awarding yourself time to be.

Your lunch bag is neatly packed and an alarm set, you have got some time right now to let loose the baggage of the day and the thoughts in your head.

You take a slow full breath, perfumed by the trees and the grass around you, you imagine that the air is like whispers, whispers of the stories born here on this bench, each breath finding its place in you.

You can feel the excitement of the dogs that have greeted their master awaiting the throw of a stick. Children with their ice creams dripping on the ground and the old man with his sandwiches wrapped in greaseproof paper.

Lovers from generations past, stealing a kiss and mothers rocking their infants in their arms.

Lost in the magical memories of your imagination, you rest with a smile on your face, knowing that you too bring whispers of stories to the bench as you drift into the memory of the first time you visited a park, wrapped in a blanket being rocked in arms, and knowing that one day, you too will be like the old man with your sandwich, lost in memory of your youth. And somehow, this bench has brought you to a place of peace, love and tranquillity.

You have a calm serenity in every cell of your body, you can feel yourself relaxing into your being, with your 'to do lists' prioritising themselves and getting into flow, your conversations being filled with ease and your strength and power returning with every gentle breath.

You take one final look around the park, the brightly coloured children and dogs racing for their sticks and you smile as you turn off your alarm and head back to your day, passing a mother with a pram and an old man with his sandwich and newspaper under his arm. You smile.

Generating The Flow Of Love

When you spend time resting in shallow waters, taking each concern, contrast or experience to this quiet space, you will begin to notice a calm contentment in your day to day life, an ability to ride the storm and rise above the problems of the world.

You might find that your relationships are healing and healthier, or it might be that you are reducing your relationships and the activities that once called you, to take more time for your spiritual growth. It might be that you are exploring different inspiring subjects and meeting new and interesting people along the way. But whatever your path, you are generating the flow of Love.

By noticing, living a more mindful life, attentive listening, observation and understanding, you have a peacefulness that floats around you, as if you are walking with feet not making contact with the earth, as if you are wearing the robes of royalty and leaving a trail of golden light behind you.

The love light that fills every cell is beginning the process of healing and as you are attracted to 'lighter' activities, relationships and nutrition, your skin becomes brighter. Letting loose the denser energies, setting you on a path to freedom and opportunity, you are glowing with the light of love.

The more regular you practise and strengthen your intention to be a beacon of light for the world, the brighter you will become. Imagine that everywhere you walk, you carry the imprint of Universal Energy impacting the world around you.

As you reflect on your learning, how far have you come in achieving moments where you are in a deep state of calm? More comfortable with silence and loving yourself enough to give yourself permission to Be?

When you are in a deep state of calm, where the deep silence lives, where your mind is at rest and you feel at one with the world. This is when you are metaphorically resting in shallow water.

SHINING BRIGHT

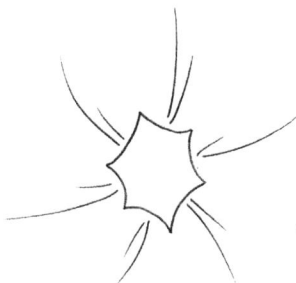

Y ou are becoming a radiant beacon of light and love and this brings you to your highest purpose: to serve. Service is a privilege and an honour when it is born of Love.

INTRODUCTION

With all of the progress you have made, you are now working with the deepest mystery of life, you are working with soul energy. Your vibrational shifts, the light that shines from you and the peace that you are feeling in your heart are evidence of your transformation. You might wonder now what to do with this light that shines within, is it just for you?

It is for the world? Each person on the planet has a role to play in the evolution of earth and the expansion of learning in All that is. Without each person, playing their role nothing would be possible: even those who you might understand to be 'outside of the light' or are offering contrast and have chosen to work on the darker side make valuable contributions. Would someone working on the dark side, actually be reading this book? Yes definitely as it will support them to understand their role in life, the contrast they bring and the decisions they made prior to birth. They too remain connected to All that Is in order to offer the contrasting vibration.

For those who are raised in a culture where all who do not conform go to Hell, I want to tell you there is no hell after death. All souls are pure essence energy and will return to All that Is. So let us look at what Hell is: it is a prison of the mind, a place where your perceived transgressions are holding you, preventing you from moving forwards and denying you your rights to freedom. It is a prison of your own making, generated by stories from history which created your culture and your experience and a prison in every negative self-effacing word you repeat to yourself.

Radiating The Energy Of Love

As you fill your body daily with the light of love, each cell vibrates and causes your body to heal. You will notice that you are unable to tolerate certain foods, drinks, films, programmes, books, locations and people. The simple reason for this is because they cause you to be out of alignment and off balance, uncomfortable, heady and ill at ease.

IF you are obligated to be in these places or with these people, it is important that you understand how to protect yourself. The very first meditation in this book began the process of bringing in the light, cleansing yourself and protecting yourself. Maintain this simple practice.

Focus On Gratitude

Prepare your day with clear intentions, bring in the light and a protective shield. Hold the vibration of love in your hand and pull it into your heart. Radiate the Light through your thoughts and send love to all including those you find difficult.

Maintain the flow of the golden thread through the breath as you complete your tasks with love and at the end of the day speak words of gratitude to your heart and soul.

Conflict

Conflict is an opportunity for growth, you know now that it is not a bad thing. Take time now to consider the 'other' and send them love even if that is through gritted teeth. You are honouring your spirit by starting with love.

Then in your imagination, float into their body to see the conflict from their perspective, feel into their lives, their culture, their education, their current life experience, their choices. See from their perspective how your view is in conflict with their own. Conflicting views are creative and enabling, should you view them as such. Equally they are destructive if you allow them to be. When you have learned all you need to, set the other free.

Forgiveness

This is one of the deepest things humans have trouble with. I am unsure why within your culture forgiveness is so hard? When you forgive, you are setting yourself free, why is that hard?

When another hurts you or your loved ones, it is right to be angry, to be hurt but revenge is a completely different thing. Hurting another because they have hurt you is nonsense. Those who hurt others may be hurt already, they may have many unhealed places within them where they chose to disconnect from all the love bestowed on them.

Retaliation or revenge will not bring you peace, your vibrational frequency is off kilter because of your thoughts, your pain, your mental anguish. Your responsibility is to restore your vibration of Love by bringing in the Light. As you know there is no darkness where there is light, so to forgive is to make way for the light and then you will be restored.

Now what do you do with the perpetrator, the person or people that have or are causing you discomfort or dis-ease? The role of the light worker is to bring light into dark places. This is the power you have inherent within you, to bring healing to the sick and light to the poor in spirit.

The Poor In Spirit

The poor in spirit are those who are disconnected from All that Is, they have travelled paths and created prisons in their minds that keep them trapped, they may have addictions, mental distress and be ill at ease in their body.

It is the role of the light worker to shine love into the dark places to enable the poor in spirit to reconnect to their source of love. They might need human kindness, food, shelter and opportunities to rebuild their lives. This is the collective responsibility, to honour the spirit within the broken and disenfranchised members of the community.

And remember to maintain your protection, to serve when you are 'filled with love' and to withdraw to restore your equilibrium. Do not run on empty.

SHINING BRIGHT

What do you need to know about becoming luminescent?
You know the story about Moses coming down from Mount Sinai after talking with God, the people described him as shining bright. Moses spoke with all the people to share the 10 commandments and they listened, and his face shone so brightly that he covered his face except when he went to speak with God.

The purpose of this book is to remove the veil, all the aspects of you that limit your potential and prevent you from living the life you desire. You will have made many changes to your life just by raising your awareness, your vibration and the thoughts that run through your mind.

Are you happy and content with your life? Are there further changes you wish to make, are you living an inspired life, a life of opportunity, a life in flow?

There are those who would rush out and make dramatic changes to their lives without having laid the groundwork. I urge you to start to live a life that you are comfortable with now, whilst you build your dreams and assimilate all the changes. In this final chapter you can review life and make powerful choices for a possible future. I am not providing you with advice about the choices you make as I don't know your history, background, culture or life experience.

When you spend time with all the practices you have learned here, life will begin to open up, the changes in you will bring opportunities your way.

Let us delve into practices which will enable you to Shine Bright: Every day open up your heart to fully live each moment. Take off your judge's wig, celebrate everything you do like a child who knows no judgement.

Start The Day With Gratitude

Breathe into every moment of your day, consciously being aware of everything you are grateful for. It could be the smallest thing or a tall building. We will use the example of the building: When you look at the building, what are you grateful for?

The person who bought the land
The person who dreamed the building
The team that financed the building
The team who pulled together to bring the dream to fruition
The architect who designed the building
The team who passed the regulations of the build
The ground workers
The builders
The people who planted & cared for the trees
The lumberjacks who cut down the trees
The sawmill that created the timbers etc

The list goes on, the more gratitude you find the greater the vibration of love fills your body, your mind and builds that connection through spirit to All that Is.

Gratitude In Relationships

If you are in relationship with people with whom you are neither grateful for or can find any gratitude for, then you can bring each person to meditation, your time of mystery and magic. These people may be playing a role that you both contracted for in order to assist growth and develop knowledge, skills and ultimately lead you both to your highest potential.

Be grateful for their lives, their purpose, their experiences that led them to where they are right now. Send them love and let all those negative feelings towards them go. Knowing that they are doing the best they can with the resources they have today. Knowing that Everything is in Perfect Order and your role in their lives is playing out perfectly.

Withdraw in whatever way you can to give yourself time to process and heal. Then the lens through which you see them will be from the source of love and you will be able to heal from any hurt they caused you.

Let gratitude be your first step in your day and be in every step throughout, then as you rest ready for sleep, put your hand on your heart, breathe in all the loveliness of the day, and think about all the lives you have touched.

The Human Body Requires Fuel

Be grateful for your gastric system that signals your body's need for nutrients, listen to your body and be guided by its call for certain foods.

As you prepare the food, handling the raw produce, be grateful for the person who tilled the land, grew the crop, harvested and processed it, the driver and the workers who got that crop to the shop workers who filled the shelves and sold the food to you. Then as you prepare to eat, pour love into it so that it nourishes your body, mind and spirit. Your body is made of water and needs water to thrive, manage hydration wisely.

The Human Body Requires Sunshine

The more time you spend in nature, in natural light the better. Be grateful for the day, whatever the weather, look up to the sky and see its majesty. Be grateful for the canopy of stars at night, the different hues of blue and white in the day and the yellows, oranges and reds of sunrise and sunset. Ever changing, infinitely magnificent and a powerful presence in your life.

Take time outside every day to walk the land, make a deep and healing connection with earth, the sand of the beach, the loam of a forest, grass and soil, be grateful for the life of earth, the shifts and changes she makes through the seasons, the lives that share her and the power held within her. Walk through forests, walk along rivers and recall all you have learned.

When you walk, breathe in the magic and mystery of the air, allow each cell to be infused with fresh air, perfumed by the land, foliage and water. Feel the air on your face and let it melt away any concerns that might leave lines there. Hold each breath for that magical moment to infuse your energy with it and know that others will breathe the same air infused with your love.

Make your walk a meditation, not the race of life, a time to slow down and observe the way the leaves are playing with the breeze, the snowdrops peeping through the ground, birdsong and the spider webs meshing the branches together.

Create stories in your mind of the lives that play out here, and hold gratitude deep in your heart for all that you see. Travel where you can in nature, explore as many different landscapes as you are able and become sensitive to the variations on earth.

The Human Body Requires Rest

Take time every day to rest and sleep, your body needs this time to heal itself and your mind requires the time to process the millions of thoughts and images it has seen throughout the day. Without rest your body and mind become exhausted and overwhelmed. This leads to illness, poor relationships and unhappiness.

What about your spirit, what does it get up to in the night? When you are sleeping you are dreaming and after the process dreams are completed your spirit is free to connect with All that Is, to receive instructions, information and to report learnings and experiences. The deep sleep will prevent you from remembering these journeys of the soul but you will be impacted by them.

As an aware and present spiritual being knowing that this is who you are, living in this body, you can use sleep time to your greatest advantage. You can request passage to the source of All that Is. You can begin the journey with your guides to 'visit' your spiritual home, your soul group and gain healing, understanding, training and to connect at soul level without the complexities of being human.

This is like Moses going up the mountain, you can do this in deep sleep or deep meditation. If you have concerns in the physical world, you can take these to your 'council' and gain guidance and advice, they will never tell you what to do as they cannot interfere with a soul incarnate on earth. But they will give you much strength to find your way.

The more time you spend in All that Is, the brighter you will shine. BUT remember, you chose to be human to have the human experience and however tempting it is to spend all day in meditation and spirit dreaming, that is not why you chose this life.

In a meditation in Drawing Back the Veil you experienced 'space travel'. You can enter this imaginary portal and create any visual process that enables you to make connections with your council.

Your council is a group of souls that you call upon for wisdom, they may be teachers, counsellors, healers, guides and higher beings, and they love you completely. Their mission is to support your lifetime as it is yours to support theirs.

When you meet with them, they will show themselves in pure form, they might be dressed in unique ways and with colours and fabrics that are unfamiliar to you. When they appear you might see them as extra terrestrial without human form, remember that you are imagining them as they wish to be imagined. If souls that you knew on earth are part of your council, they will show themselves as the animals or humans you recognise if that suits them, but not always.

Your council are the fundamental pillar of your life here on earth, they will support you to remove any limiting beliefs and open your mind to great creativity. They will not all 'turn up' when you call a meeting, only the members who have the skills and gifts you need. You can use any of the guided meditations to make contact with them and it is perfectly Ok to talk to any member at any time.

When you 'meet' yourself in soul form for the first time, it can be quite overwhelming. On earth you might see yourself as small and insignificant, when in actual fact you are far from either of those concepts. You are magnificent, powerful and extraordinary. The gifts you possess, the capacity for love you hold shine through you, the more you unveil yourself of those small images and beliefs about yourself the more you will shine.

Can you start living life here on earth in this body with all of your magnificence? A resounding yes and that is what you are called to do. To expand the energetic frequency of earth by sharing this incredible vibration that emanates from you. The vibration of love, of healing, joy, peace, fun, knowledge, wisdom and compassion.

The moment you start believing this, others will notice the changes in you. The magic and mystery that is you becomes attractive to others, your eyes shine brightly and your energetic frequency is like a magnet. Use this new frequency in conjunction with the law of attraction, making sure that your desires align with your dreams and it will help you determine your purpose.

The Law Of Attraction

There is much written about attraction and I want to share all I understand about this in order that you use it wisely. The more you engage in thinking about something the more likely it is that you will receive that which you desire. If you think in the negative, it is as powerful as you think in the positive. Therefore you must truly consider what you are thinking.

Shining Bright: if you have met your highest potential in All that Is and experienced what it feels like to be powerful, but on earth you are still feeling small, you might be saying something like, "that's just not me, I am not that important, there is no way I could be that powerful here on earth"

The "Law of Attraction" will be listening and will respond accordingly by giving you what you are asking for is exactly that: Powerlessness. When you set intentions, you are sending signals to your unconscious which communicates with your conscious brain and focusing on the intention leads to attracting those elements into your life. It is important therefore to bring the reality of your magnificence to the surface and believe in the magic of you every day.

The Seeds Of The Dream

Take time every day to dream, to think about the life you desire, how it looks, how it feels, who is in it, where it is, how all of your experience has led you to the dream.

Create powerful images of yourself in this dream, walk over into the image to gather all the information you need. Work out who is already in your life who will support your dream and those who have professional skills who can guide you towards it. If you allow your dream to be 'unlimited', really play with it, imagine the car of your desire gliding down a rural street in some far off place towards the mansion where you live, with your_____ and your ____.

Like painting by numbers just keep filling the image and smelling the roses, the air, the trees, the wonderful food cooking, the laughter of the people there having fun. Notice what you notice and feel what you feel.

At the end of the dream session, evaluate it. What was important and why? The seeds of the dream are here. The dream car might have to wait because that is only a possession, what did you learn about the rest of the dream and this is where you can start.

If for example you want to eat really wonderful food, then maybe join a cookery course where other people are dreaming the same dream. Learn to cook wonderful food and when you are able, invite friends round and recreate the dream of having all those people having fun around your table.

When we trust our highest potential, to guide us through dreaming, we increase the chances of meeting the people we want to meet and living the life we dreamt of.

Trusting Our Highest Potential

The more time we spend in All that Is, learning about ourselves, our guides, our council and others, the more we build a powerful relationship with our soul energy or Highest Potential. We can call upon this guidance to show us the way to demystify concerns, to become limitless, to power up our compassion, our gifts and to lead us to our purpose.

Every day, spend time with your highest potential, listening, learning, opening up to your feelings, being able to communicate your fears, your joys and celebrate your achievements. In this process you will grow in strength, shine brightly and good things will follow you.

Celebrating Life

When you live with a passion for life, for love, for nature, earth and creation, there is a lightness that follows, a skip in the step, and ease of flow. This is the path of source energy running through you and guiding you.

You will find that the more you make the connection by plugging into All that Is, you will discover your unique voice of expression. This can be exhilarating and magnetic for you, and although I wouldn't discourage you from this work, I will say that unless you are called to monastic life, there is much living to do. It is in both action and living that the true work is created.

A Simple Routine

Morning and Evening in your sacred space of mystery, spread the light of love from earth and the universe to all.

Practice gratitude throughout the day, blessing your food and drink and making conscious decisions to be grateful for every experience. Saying thank you to people who support you in both large and small ways. Listen with your heart to the people you meet and speak from your heart and share your wisdom and offer guidance on request.

Hold space for world issues and those you know who are in distress and if you love journaling, then allow your highest wisdom to speak to you through the written word.

The Lens Of Love

Are you beginning to see how the lens you choose to look at any situation changes the view? Do you understand how you can easily shift your thoughts by changing your lens?

We know that the lens through which we see the world is generated from nature, nurture, geography, experience with others, your hobbies, interests and passions all change the lens and come with a critical bias.

If your lens is 'health and fitness' the criticism may be of people who are overweight or inactive. If your lens is of 'learning' the criticism may be of those who are uneducated or those who pretend they are. The list goes on and I wonder if you can see how your hobbies, passions and interests seen through the lens of love become unique and beautiful to you without the bias of criticism for those who don't follow your path?

There is much to learn about yourself through these simple exercises and writing your observations down will support your own personal and spiritual development.

I have told you that when I was working to heal the sick, the people all held up a very destructive lens, they saw dark evil everywhere and fear was their primary lens believing that the Gods will smite you if you..... When I worked with them to heal their ailments, I shared the truth with them and although they couldn't disclose this information to others, those that embraced the truth were healed and went on to become wisdom keepers, healers and prophets.

Healing requires commitment and perseverance and a willingness to make changes in your life.

HEALING

When you shine bright this does not preclude you from sickness, the physical world is enhanced by your presence and connection to All that Is and will support faster healing, however there is a need to take responsibility for your health.

Simple Steps To Maintain Health And Wellbeing

I will not tell you what to do as I don't know your culture or physical needs, use this simply as a prompt and allow your intuition to teach you when you are in mystery. If you are unwell, seek support from specialists in that field. On a day to day basis, taking responsibility for your health requires simple steps:

Caring for the body:

What you put into it, what you do with it and how you treat it.

Caring for the mind:

Your thoughts, what you feed your mind, and with whom you listen and are influenced by.

Caring for your spirit:

Taking time in mystery, learning and sharing with others and building your tribe.

Once you have your body, mind and spirit in alignment with health and wellbeing, you find peace and notice small changes and improvements in overall wellbeing and quality of life. You might begin to notice patterns of health and be able to make further adjustments. You might find yourself drawn to learning more about the body, studying it, understanding what it needs.

Allow this process to flow, it is inspired and important work, take time, no rush, go gently and learn to completely love your body, the way it moves, the touch of your skin and the times when it feels energised. Notice the beauty of your mind as you mindfully wander through nature, as you enter into debate or create new and exciting things. And grow with your spirit as you let loose layers of conditioning and as you practise forgiveness to release you from pain.

Your body is a temple, a place of great beauty, a vehicle of your humanity. It might not be beautiful by worldly standards which are popularised and false. Your body is magnificent and it's magical qualities are amazing.

When you seek a healthy lifestyle, it's because you want to preserve your body for as long as you can, so that you can fulfil your life's purpose. It doesn't matter if your body is broken or old, or pained - it matters that you do all you can to maintain it.

When it comes to healing, there are many modalities that I used:

I used the Ankh as a vibrational tool to match the energies to health.
I used universal energy and earth energy to infuse the cells
I used poultices, bindings, tinctures & syrups
I wrapped sores and ulcers in leaves, used hot and cold compresses and manipulated the flesh to move stuck energy
I was limited in knowledge of the day but called upon my council to assist me.
I raised people from the dead
I gave people their sight
I healed the broken hearted
I assisted people in transitioning from this life
I used song and music to raise the spirits
I used love as a cure all

There is a magic in your hands that you can use to support yourself and others to heal, this is healing energy through the golden thread that you bring through you with intention as love radiates through you to their body and creates the process of healing.

Simple Steps To Healing

First open your mind to the possibility that sickness is a form of stuck energy, energy that cannot move because of fear. Fear shows up in the body in many ways, stress, anxiety, depression, anger, worry and hatred. Fear is generated at a conscious level, in your mind that repeats the story over and over again. There may have been a trigger or many triggers for this fear that was a real experience but you survived that experience.

Constant repetitive recounting of the events builds up fear resistance in the body which generates sickness. By taking time out to process the triggers enables you to examine how and where you are generating blockages. Find a practice that enables you to unwrap these stories buried deep inside of your conscious mind. Here are a few ideas: Writing out your thoughts without thinking about what you are writing. Speaking your truth to yourself when walking in nature and alone. Setting your intentions to clear a repeated concern whilst you sleep and calling on your guides to help the process.

Create a log of repeated statements and processes that keep you stuck and work through them one at a time. If a person is part of the story: Make a decision now to forgive them and set yourself free. As you clear thought after thought a lightness will come to you, this lightness has a vibrational energy that supports healing and you will find clarity and a positive state of mind that will also aid healing.

Discovering The Power Of Health

We have established that good health is a daily responsibility to make healthy choices, to find balance and to take time in mystery to flood yourself with healing light.

No amount of energetic healing is going to rebuild a lost limb, however the power of the mind can remove limitations of living without a limb. There are many who live with profound sickness and physical limitation, yet they have perfect calm. They find great happiness and joy in their lives and a deep contentment.

These people have made a deep connection with their highest potential, their soul energy. They understand their purpose and are living it without judgement. They may be serving all those who support their daily lives and bodily functions, by emitting their light energy and sending love. They have a deep contentment with all they have and don't regret what they have not or aren't able to have. They choose life in this body, in this version of now.

When you look in the mirror, look at your eyes, are they bright and shining? Look at your skin, is it healthy and glowing? And your hair, is it glossy and full? These are the signs of health that you can work on.

I would often bathe people who were sick, gently cleansing their bodies, using oils and tinctures, to restore their skin, to help them to glow, to shine. Washing their hair and deeply massaging their scalp to release stuck energies. Body massage and clearing all the stuck energies by pulling through the feet, deeply massaging their feet between their toes and heels.

Encouraging them to self care, to self love and to accept that their beauty lay deep inside them and this body is their vehicle of life here, a life they chose. Asking them if they were willing to change any aspect of their life to restore them to health and offering them to consider a new direction towards full health and restoration.

There is no judgement in All that Is, if you choose the path of sickness and ultimate transition back to soul energy.

There is a path to follow that you set before birth, if you change your mind, there will be other life opportunities for you to experience the same opportunities again.

Transition From This Life

This human experience is finite, your body will be left behind when it is your time to transition. There is nothing to fear in this experience, it will be as if you unzip yourself from this body and return home. Like an actor taking off their disguise and returning home at the end of the evening performance.

There is no such place as hell, except maybe the place in your mind where you tell yourself fearful stories. All souls return home and their experiences are valued without judgement.

Home is a place of great beauty and comfort, there will be much celebration as you are received back into your soul family. You will wander through all of your experiences on earth and extract the learning from them and then decide what your next learning will be. Time in Source Energy is not linear and is not measured as it is on earth. Your soul will spend a great deal of time learning and teaching from this life experience.

Grief

When loved ones transition, it is painful and emotional, all hopes and plans of the imagined future life are closed down and the feelings are powerful and a deep sadness comes upon you. Grieving in my culture was public and physical, with much wailing and communicated despair. Allowing this physical release without holding back, we cared for our dead and prepared them for their return. All these practices were our way of honouring our loved ones.

Allow as much time as you need to grieve, do it your way but don't stop living. Your loved one would want you to live the best life, to continue your path and to lean on all the beauty of your shared life. And know that their energy remains with you, that connection is always there for you to draw on.

I want you to imagine what your soul looks like when you remove your body suit. Every step you have taken on this journey here has been about releasing the radiant divine light that is you. The light that glows from you and draws people to you, The light that lights up the room when you walk in and the light that shuns the darkness by your presence.

This light is pure golden light, so bright it shines white to the naked eye. This light is pure beauty, pure love, pure innocence and unfiltered love.

Shine Bright that you might shine for all to see that they too might be transformed by all you are.

Healing Others

It's really important to heal yourself, you do not need to be completely healed or be completely whole before you start sharing your wisdom.

Many people believe that they are nothing and that the little bit of knowledge they have is insufficient to start sharing with other people. Can I tell you that every single element of you has a story to tell that will help another. It's how you choose to live your life and shine your light that will show people the magic and mystery of you and when they are amazed by you, intrigued by you or curious about you, that is when you get the opportunity to share your wisdom.

Wisdom is that knowledge embedded deep within each cell of your body. It radiates out, having been processed by your life, your thoughts and by your experiences. Here is the evidence of your transformation, how you have unveiled yourself of many limitations, how you have grown, in your own way, in the direction of your dreams, and how the Love light radiates through and from you.

Now you are able to share this wisdom and when

people see your light and are drawn to it and ask what you have done to create such profound change. You will be able to share your knowledge and guide others in the direction of their dreams by unveiling their own magic.

When you shine bright, there is a desire to help others seek their own light, to shake off their limiting beliefs and life experience that has caused them to cower, to hide and to limit their world view. There is a passion rising within you for the world, to see each person functioning wonderfully, to wake up to the magnificence of each other, to seek opportunities for joy and a deep meaningful sense of happiness.

You will become a champion of the light, not necessarily by the words you speak but by the light that emanates from your very being - which will transform the room and the people within it. Just by being in your presence being the person you are, so highly connected to All that Is, divinity is running through your body and through each cell so that when you breathe in the golden light and breathe out the golden thread you are channelling healing.

When you are in mystery, you can bring people to mind, people who you want to reach and who at this moment in time may not be ready to hear your words. You can touch their hearts and souls in mystery using the golden thread. As you breathe out the love that you've pulled in from All that Is and fill yourself with radiant golden light, direct it in your mind to the people who you are holding in your thoughts, it may be for healing, freedom, transformation, strength, or just holding space. The degree to which they will receive this pure light will be in direct correlation to their free will. You have intuited their need but you are not controlling how they receive the energy that you're sending them. That is not your role, it's not necessary for you to know it's only necessary that you send the love to them with a pure heart and a pure mind.

One of the greatest gifts you can give to people is an opportunity to be heard, your role to be able to listen without judgement or need to provide solutions. To listen without desire beyond their desire for transformation. When you listen you must listen with your heart wide open not just with your ears, you must listen with your eyes to see the love in that person to see them already whole again.

One of the other gifts you can give people is the gift of your experience and your story, do not labour, keep to the key points that might support their needs. This will help them to feel at ease and to know that you have some idea what they're going through.

Holding space is an expression of a silence that you can be in with that person and it might be that that silence is physically with them or just holding that silence within yourself on their behalf. So if you are walking into a room where somebody is sick do not bombard them with your knowledge, skills and wisdom just sit and hold their hand if that is appropriate or just be in their energy field if not, offer comfort and make that connection with their divinity.

Bear witness to their experience without judgement or expectation. Hold space for them as their body makes choices to heal and know that your healing presence and the vibration you bring will support their body to realign to wellbeing, even if this is to transition.

When your loved one is sick it is very hard to separate emotions and not enter into a mental dialogue about the possible outcome of this sickness, especially if they have a label assigned by a medical person. Medicine predominantly deals with the physiology of the human body, removing, correcting, or stitching back together but healing is not the primary component of Modern medicine.

How the mind chooses to interpret the diagnosis will impact on the outcome of the illness. Healing is dependent on your physical body merging with your spiritual body and your spiritual life path to manage the conscious mind which otherwise would get stuck in fear.

Therefore, your role as an informal healer, one who is using intention and access to All that Is, requires only intention. You can encourage the sick person to raise their vibration in alignment with earth, you can do this by bringing that higher vibration into the room and filling them with Radiant Golden Light, when they feel loved in this way, your calm and beautiful energy will raise theirs to match it. We are not expanding on this greatly in this first book as there is far more to learn about being a healer in book 2, however you have all that is necessary to support people to realign their vibration and to hold space for them to heal.

One of the things you can do for the sick person on the road to recovery is to support their journey of health. Aristotle suggested that you ask the sick person "Are you willing to give up that which made you sick?"

This provides a benchmark to whether or not the person would be willing to make life changes to promote healing. These changes might be in the mind, their actions or activity, the words they speak and the attitude towards their life. One can view sickness as being out of alignment with your soul and earth energy.

When sickness strikes it is necessary to review your needs: Physical needs: Air, Breath, Fluids, Movement, Nutrition, Rest, Sleep. Mental Health needs: Calm, Connection, Creativity, Peace, Stimulation, Time, Quiet.Spiritual needs: Meditation, Mindfulness, Nature, Soul connection, Vibrational Alignment with the Frequency of Love.

Stress which is a great cause of sickness can cause a rift or break in connection to health and wellbeing, generated through an internal dialogue or external circumstance, creating burnout. One might see burnout as a bowl with holes in it - like a colander, although the person is bringing the golden light through the golden thread and the radiant golden light from earth, it is expelled immediately.

Introduce the person who is unwell to oxygenate their body, they might be receiving oxygen or it might be that they need to change and modify their breathing. Breathwork will help calm and reconnect the person to the vibration of earth.

You can teach them by modelling the breath, ask them to breathe with you and as they breathe you can share with them elements from your journey of transformation that relates to their own journey. As you create a beautiful healing rhythm of the breath and you encourage that person to breathe regularly in this beautiful way then their body stands a great chance of healing. As they breathe, you can fill yourself with love light and cover them in love and if they are open you can share one of the meditations in this book.

Encourage the sick person to drink water, infuse this filtered water with earth energy, sunlight or moonlight and add crystals to support healing. Tell a story of life giving water encouraging imagination to see each precious drop filling each cell and restoring health, or shrinking a tumour if that is necessary.

You can also massage their feet, if they're unable to have their feet massaged or don't like their feet being touched then you can massage their hands. When you are touching the person make sure that it is a gentle touch using cream or an oil to really work into their feet, and if you've studied reflexology then use these principles to support healing.

When you massage the hands or the feet, bring your love into that process, imagine the golden light coming through your hands into the feet and entering each cell of their body.

When I healed people, I used my Ankh which was a tuning fork with the vibration of health and healing, I would place the Ankh on their greatest point of need, their heart for emotional problems, their spine for strength, their knees for direction and their head for freedom from the mental torture they were putting themselves through.

I also used crystals, different crystals from my land that I would just pick up and sometimes they were just stones but I would infuse them with love and I would infuse them with health and wellbeing and I would often leave these stones or crystals underneath people's pillows in pockets or laying on top of them.

When you are offering healing like this to your friends and your family who are sick they will receive only what their spirit allows. Life is mapped out and although you have free will, the contracts you made will end and your life in this body will end. Healing can take many forms including a peaceful release from this earthly body.

Vibrational Energy

I have spoken before of the people that I served and how they lived in fear of some terrible catastrophe, that they would be smited by the Gods and thought they were under surveillance and any misdemeanour would lead them to harsh sanctions and possibly death.

Living with fear creates vulnerability, division and far greater risk than those who chose to live their lives without fear. Fear is a very dense energy, as heavy as lead and as malleable as clay. It morphs into strange creatures, dark paths and clings like moss. It is a virus that grows daily, completely destroying movement, laughter, love and creativity. It is painful and exhausting and leads to sickness and ultimately death. It is a construct of the mind, it expands with every thought until the fearful are cloaked completely in it.

You Shine Bright when the cloak of fear is removed, you are free to move, to love, to laugh, to dance, to sing. Creativity spills out of each cell, the world is bright, positive and wholesome. You face difficulty with an objective ease, acknowledging the problem, your own responsibility in it (if this is the case) and you seek solutions and reparation.

Shining Bright means that you can face adversity with internal power and calm. When you operate from a place of love, your vibrational energy is effervescent. It is light and free and attractive for all to see. You glow from that deeper inner place of knowing. You flow through the day with ease, you face battles by shining your light of love onto those who would choose to battle with you. You can read between the lines, you can read the other's energy and know what limitation is creating this conflict. You can shine your light deeply into their lives and gently remove yourself from the conflict.

Maintaining your vibrational energy of light requires a commitment to choosing the lens of love whatever is happening around you. It is easy to see the fears, the hardships, the propaganda, the traps and limitations of a hard path. By embracing the belief that Everything is in Perfect Order enables you to maintain your vibration of Light and observe the event objectively.

Objectivity does not necessitate making a judgement about those caught up in fear, or those who are generating fear. Objectivity allows you to be free of any fearful realities that your peers are experiencing. You can stand back, stand firm, stand strong and hold yourself in the Light with the lens of Love.

Managing your vibration whilst being fully participant in the world requires a daily choice.

Simple Steps

Follow whatever daily routine you have created, to enter into mystery. Go as deep as you are able, to that place of calm serenity where you experience an understanding that Everything is in Perfect Order.

Invite your guides, angels, beings and loved ones to join you in a circle of light and speak to you about the situation. Bring to them any fears you have for your safety and ask for guidance about any action you are considering.

Each being will offer you guidance based on their gifts and relationship with you. The architect will explain what is happening, the planner will explain why and the guide will shine golden light on possible paths so you can see where they lead and be able to make a choice. The nurturer will hold you and remind you of your power and the joker will tease you and bring light energy to eradicate any fears.

When you have completed the meditation, return and write in your journal. Allow all you have learned to assimilate before taking action. You may wish to raise the vibration of your planet in order that this will destroy the darkness. When you are ready to serve the world in this way and from wherever you are starting this journey - everything you choose to do will be of value.

Simple Steps

Enter into mystery and bring in golden light through the golden thread. Breathe in and out through your heart and feel the vibrational shift within your body and spreading out into the world. Allow the light to cleanse and heal everything it touches, people, homes, trees, flowers, animals. Breathe the radiant golden light in from the centre of earth, through your root at the base of your spine. This heart energy of earth is very powerful , breathe in and flood your body all the way to your head and allow a stream of light to rise out of you directing it upwards.

Earth's energy will then merge with All that Is and create a dome of protection. Within this dome, the vibrational energy of the planet will rise. Bring yourself back into presence.

Return to this meditation daily and see the power rising through you and impacting your life and all those around you.

Situations Outside Of Your Control

The vibrational frequency of individuals, groups, cultures and locations will impact upon the collective. If you are in a place where the energy is fearful, however fear is generated or understood, then there are strategies that you can use to protect yourself and others.

Simple Step To Protection

Preparing for Mystery:

Time: Choose how much time you can spend, ensuring that all your responsibilities are cared for and that you have time to complete any tasks. You do not want to bring anxiety about time into this space. Set yourself a time limit and ask your guides to keep you to this. Set an alarm if you are learning to trust your guides.

Intention: Make clear your intention and anchor that into a crystal, a stone or into a mudhra or hand shape. If this intention is for another, bring their face to mind and begin by sending them love and surrounding them with light. Repeat this for each person you wish to bring into this time of mystery. If it is a collective, then bring the crowd and surround them with light.

Breath & Imagination: Bring the light of love in through the Golden Thread on each breath, breathe into your upper heart and allow the light to flood you. When every cell in your body is full and you feel that vibrational shift then fill your auric field, extend this out to all that you have brought with you until they are encased in the golden light and each of their cells are vibrating in harmony. Imagine that each person has their own sound and that the music you are hearing sounds beautiful to your ears.

Protection: As you both or all stand together surrounded by the light of love, call in your guides, angels, loved ones and council. Call in the guides and angels of others in your intention and all universal energies available to create a dome of protection around you. Imagine this dome as a physical structure made of glass, metal, crystal etc and see how everyone under this dome is bathed in golden light.

Petition: Communicate your needs to the protectors and trust them to support you. Ask for guidance, direction or ways to present yourself to the world to ensure yours and others safety.

Bring yourself back to the sacred space, stretch and hydrate and as you gently go about your day, keep anchoring the image of protection into your being to keep fear at bay.

AND FINALLY

At this stage of your transformation, the light that emanates from you is a manifestation of the inner world that you have transformed, the stories you have rewritten and the goals you have achieved.

When people see you, radiant and at peace, they will feel your energy and be in wonder which might spark a desire for their own transformation. .

As you look at them with the lens of love you will see their light within and a desire to fill them with Universal Light. You will become a bright and shiny mirror for them to see their reflection. As you believe in their magnificence, as you find their hidden gems they too will begin to see that they are not the story they have told themselves for so long that they believe it to be the truth.

Some people will not like their reflection, finding that changing their mind seems far too big a mountain to climb. In this case, do not labour, trust that they will seek transformation in their own good time, just like you did. Know deep inside you that they are not rejecting you, they are rejecting their possible transformation.

You can still fill them with love in the full knowledge that their highest wisdom and All that Is will be grateful and the seeds sown here will flourish one day.

The more you seek beauty in people, the more you will shine, there will be no limit to the love that flows through you, healing you and the very ground you walk on.

When you are not shining bright, the law of attraction will bring mirrors towards you to show you how to transform the next step in your life.

In this exciting adventure called Life, you will come

across thousands of people, and each time you meet them, your vibrational energy, your light and your love will impact each one. Send them love, send them forgiveness and light the path before them when you get the opportunity.

If you are walking down the road and see something that concerns you, even if you are unable to take action, you can shower the situation with the Radiant Golden Light of Earth and call in angels and guides to support.

It is my deepest hope that you are now shining your light for all to see, that you are maintaining a higher vibration and living an abundant and powerful life.

Choice

When you Shine Bright, you look at life with the lens of curiosity, this lens colours everything with a shimmer. Ordinarily people tend to see things in black and white and although you have suspended much of your judgement going through this journey of transformation, there is a lifetime's work to do. You will know when your journey is over, because you will leave this body behind.

If your life was supposed to be dull and you were supposed to be dulled, then this opportunity would not have come to you. Are you curious about that? The reason you found this book, the reason that this or that happened, all led you to this very magical moment of now. Without all of these synchronicities, accidents, opportunities, connecting with strangers you would not be here right now. Isn't that curious?

When you choose the lens of curiosity - it inspires creativity. You look out on a bright and sunny day and you wonder, what next? What will life throw at you today, what amazing opportunities will come your way, what will you find along this path, where does that path lead etc. Can you feel the vibrational energy that is generated just by the questions that you have asked in your mind when reading this?

You equally look out on a dark and dull day, maybe it's raining and cloudy outside and inside. With the lens of curiosity you are likely to pull out the most amazing opportunities, to sit with that book you have longed to read, to pull out those craft items you have been waiting to create with. To take a lazy bath or sort out those cupboards.

Life is all about choice, what you choose to make of it and the simplest way to do this, is to put on the Lens of Curiosity.

Curiosity

Is this different from being nosy? Yes it is,when you look at a person you are looking at them with great love, wondering what you could learn from them or share with them. You are admiring them for whatever reason you noticed them.

If you noticed something that led you to put the judge's wig back on, that person might be a mirror to show you your own 'judgement' and your own 'unhealed place'.

If you notice their hurt, anger, sadness, then you are noticing their unhealed places, and how do you know that this is what you are seeing? because you are remembering your own unhealed places.

Do you see the value of curiosity in your life? How can you extend this lens of curiosity to serve others?

Once you suspend judgement you can reach into the hearts and minds of man, adding the lens of love to the fundamental belief that all humans are made from love, that they are valuable and necessary for harmonious functions of the planet, then you can shine your light upon them.

In the understanding and belief that Everything is in Perfect Order and that All is Good in All that Is, you cannot fail but to serve. Not because of your words, just by your presence.

The light that shines from you, is honest, full of integrity, compassionate, kind and filled with love. The need to be right, the need to control and the need to punish have no place in your life and you radiate the golden light of love, leaving a trail wherever you go.

When you sense another's pain, you can quietly and gently pour love into them, when you hear another's anger, you can pour love into them, you can hold space for everyone, knowing that they are working it out, doing their best with the resources they hold.

If you are called to use your knowledge, skills or gifts in a helping capacity, then filling yourself with radiant golden light as you serve others, will empower you and your gifts that you share.

We have come to the end of the first step in our journey, it is time now to reward yourself with a time of assimilation, absorbing all that you have learned and allowing your body, mind and spirit to align. Awakenings are exciting and exhilarating, but without taking time to reflect and find your balance in life, you will lose the power of your work.

The glue that holds you together, that links body, mind and spirit is Love. It is impossible to live fully, wholly, completely without Love.

ACKNOWLEDGEMENT

With deepest gratitude to all who have so generously given of their time and knowledge to support the writing and publication of this book. And with humility we honour YOU for the work you have done throughout, to unveil the magic of you. It is our greatest wish that you continue on the journey of transformation and see where it leads.

ABOUT THE AUTHOR

Susi Jones

Susi has devoted her life to the care of people with challenging life experiences, working professionally both as clinician and manager in mental health services and beyond. She specialises in assisting people to restore their strength and belief in themselves and to discover their own innate power of healing.

Now working as a hypnotherapist and NLP practitioner in private practice and offering Isis Healing Codes and Intutive readings online and in person.

Susi is a gifted healer and channel who began working with Goddess Isis in January 2021 to bring knowledge and wisdom to a world in flux.

This is the first of three books Isis wishes to share with the world

BOOKS BY THIS AUTHOR

Companion Journal: Isis Wisdom Unveiling The Magic Of You

Companion Journal to record your progress on your journey of transformation

ISBN: 978-0-9930824-3-6

Sleep Cards

A pack of sleep cards written and produced by Susi Jones under the title Healthy in Mind.
48 beautiful sleep cards to guide you gently into a healthy, healing sleep.

ISBN: 978-0-9930824-0-5

Printed in Great Britain
by Amazon